LIVING INNER DEVELOPMENT

Living Inner Development

The Necessity of True Inner Development
in the Light of Anthroposophy

LISA ROMERO

SteinerBooks | 2016

SteinerBooks
An imprint of Anthroposophic Press, Inc.
610 Main Street, Great Barrington, MA 01230
SteinerBooks.org

PRINT: 978-1-62148-152-2
eBook: 978-1-62148-153-9

CONTENTS

Introduction

Although we may all have our personal preferences of understanding what constitutes a good life for ourselves, if we scratch the surface of all ways of living, there seems to be an unavoidable recognition that life is also about growth and development. We need only look at the reality of what has taken place in the world around us. If life is not about growth and development, why have we as a collective humanity invested so much in advancing the various levels of the human experience?

We can also see this principle of growth and development in the unfolding of each individual human being. The attributes that differentiate us from the animal kingdom can be perceived as an element of this: no other mammal takes twenty years to come to maturity. And after twenty years, this process of maturity and growth only ceases in an outer sense. Inwardly, the human being continues to seek to change, develop, and grow in mind or task or experience. What in us truly needs to grow? The human being evolves, and we participate in human evolution by participating in our own development.

We can do nothing more helpful for the world's further evolution than to evolve ourselves. This is something that, in fact, we must do. And we have no doubt whatsoever that we *must*, the moment we perceive the truth about our own nature and its relationship with the wider world.[1]

Spiritual development allows us to recognize, and to participate in, the evolution "willed by the gods." In the course of inner development, spiritual development, the human being crosses the threshold between physical reality and spiritual reality. In the experiences unfolded there, the human being takes on within itself the evolution willed by the higher guiding forces. Without this kind of inner development, humanity might only develop in ways willed by other active forces such as materialism and egotism.

By developing ourselves further, we actively contribute—though in small measure—to the evolution willed by the gods.[2]

There are three ways, other than through the death of the body, in which the human being may cross the threshold between the sense world and that realm which is imperceptible to sensory experience: We can cross into this world through an *inner training*, by means of which the human being develops a readiness to enter into new states of consciousness and to meet what is to be found in this other realm. We can also cross the threshold, although in an altered way, by means of *toxicity or trauma* to the bodily sheaths. And thirdly, at the present time we can be susceptible to crossing in the sense that humanity *as a whole* is beginning to undergo a premature crossing of the threshold, for in our age the threshold is being drawn closer to us.

Each way of crossing bears its own results for the development of the individual, and thus, for the development of the collective consciousness. In the small contribution that follows, we will explore various experiences of these three possibilities of crossing the threshold. By recognizing what we are experiencing in each of the various realms of the spiritual world that we encounter upon crossing, we will come to better understand these realms themselves.

Many esoteric schools have given teachings that serve the students of the spirit in their process of development. However comprehensive the teachings may be, in the end we are essentially alone in summoning the effort required of us in order to develop and to evolve ourselves individually and consciously. We must be our own guides to a large extent as we travel the inner work path; however, in order to understand not only our own experiences but also the experiences of others, we need to be able to evaluate where we are. How can we individualize and take up what comes through the wisdom of the inner schooling, and yet not 'play' with the wisdom and alter it in a way that removes its transformative power—or worse yet, in a way that makes of it a *diversion* from the truth?

When, many years ago, I asked my anthroposophical teacher, "Why this path, what makes it so special?"—as I had already been exposed to both Western and Eastern teachings—he replied, "Yes, you may have come across many of these things in other teachings, but to my knowledge (Erwin was a researcher of these things) no other school has given such a comprehensive understanding of the spiritual worlds. It is through anthroposophy that we may understand and shed light on all other paths." Increasingly, I have recognized the truth of what he shared.

This book is not only an attempt to reiterate, from another way of experience, the path of the spirit that has already been given by many. It is also an attempt to help us make sense, *from the perspective of the student of the inner work*, of the experiences we encounter in ourselves and the world as our inner lives develop on this path. Many who are striving to make headway on the path are experiencing encounters with other realms of consciousness. And many who strive do so out of a recognition of the necessity of spiritual development.

This work is meant as a support to the independence of our individual journey, and, at the same time, it is meant to enkindle reverence for the majesty and mystery of the inner training that has been gifted by the great initiates, through their ability to work with the guiding progressive beings who walk with us. As we are not great initiates, and as so much therefore lies concealed from each of us, we do require esoteric schooling in order that we can recognize the truth along the path we will walk.

Although we must travel our paths independently, it is an esoteric truth that *by ourselves* we cannot lift the veil that conceals the hidden worlds from us. Inwardly and/ or outwardly, we will need the help of others at all stages of our training.

Knowing how we can influence others, it is important to understand not only each aspect of the human being that must undergo change on the path of inner development, but also how we can assist others on their journey towards development. "The future of spiritual-esoteric movements such as ours will depend more and more upon the realization that human spiritual development is necessary."[3]

Supporting others requires that we ourselves have awoken to certain truths and capacities. Unfortunately, or fortunately, this is the living reality of inner development. As Rudolf Steiner said to the teachers—and this applies to us all on this path—(to paraphrase): *It is not what you know, but who you are that is important.*[4]

Of course, it is a big request to make of any human being that they walk the path of transformation so that they may be of true assistance to the other. *But it must become a matter of individual recognition to know that I can only truly help if my eyes have been awoken and my ears can hear.* The call to self-development is a call to world-development. Anthroposophy is this call, and for no other reason is its existence justified.

If anthroposophical spiritual science were ever to be given a mantle suitable for the atmosphere of coffee-parties or what corresponds to them nowadays, this would by no means be conducive to the fulfillment of its task—for this task is one of pressing urgency. The reason for the hostility that is asserting itself at the present time in such ugly forms is simply this: People realize that here it is not a matter of a sect, or of a happier 'family circle' such as many desire, but that something is truly striving to activate the impulses needed by our times.[5]

Many people are expressing this feeling of urgency and of how it is essential that more of humanity awaken to a recognition of living with spiritual realities. Steiner frequently stated that in the 20th century, humanity as a whole would begin to cross the threshold. This process has begun; we can already see its negative results through the increase in psychiatric disorders—manifesting, for example, in the extreme prevalence of depression and anxiety. On the other hand, we can also recognize the positive consequences of crossing the threshold, in the speed with which the world is changing and the unprecedented rate at which new ideas, thoughts, and insights are able to flourish. This may not be what we expected to see as a result of the diminishing of the veil dividing the sense world and the spiritual world, but these are all marks of humanity's changing relationship to these worlds.

This book is the third in a sequence of books written to support inner development. In this book, the student of the work will need some background in anthroposophy or some inner experience of the path. It presupposes the knowledge of the meditative practice as described in the previous book, *The Inner Work Path: Foundations of Meditative Practice in the Light of Anthroposophy*. However, as with all inner work writings, it is accessible to those who can utilize it. Through entering into the content of this book's outline of the path of initiation, we can understand not only our own path and where we are on it, but also the path of others and the support others may need. We will be able to understand why certain things in the world are becoming more popular and how we can participate in working alongside the collective journey towards the good.

I

Inner Development
for the Physical World

In an understanding of how the human being develops and evolves in each aspect of self allows insight into every stage of human growth. There is the growth of the outer body, the development of the mind, and the awakening awareness of the spirit, of the true self. Before we enter into the detail of each of these in the following chapters, it is useful to describe the overview of their evolution from the point of view of one aspect of esotericism and its terminology.

The inner development path outlined throughout anthroposophical literature is designed to support the understanding of spiritual worlds, and not to generate mere belief in, or give mere information about, these realms. Rather, this given body of work seeks to begin to school students in the direction of understanding these worlds for themselves.

Each individual must tread the path of inner development for themselves, simply because it is by walking this path that the healthy faculties required for perceiving the spiritual world are to be attained. In some ways this gives us the enthusiasm to guide our own way, knowing that we ourselves are responsible for the journey. Yet without the map given by the great initiates, we could easily apply our materialistic-intellectual thinking to the inner work, which would lead us away from any true knowledge.

Even when a clear map is given, many mistakes can occur due to the ordinary intellect's inability to understand spiritual realities. Recently, speaking at a conference in New York City, a highly regarded international meditation scholar suggested to the audience that lucid dreaming was the same as what is known on the meditative path as a "continuity or continuation of consciousness,"[6] and advised that the participants should buy books on lucid dreaming if they wanted to understand what the traditions mean by the experience of the continuity of consciousness. Unfortunately, he made a serious error— one that is misleading for true inner development and that would misdirect the student if given as advice.

It is true that certain words may be used to describe lucid dreaming which are also used to describe a continuity of consciousness. It is necessary to use words; we must do so in order to relay spiritual experiences to the other. But these experiences cannot be taken in the same way as earthly experiences.

For example, a four-year-old child might play with a cardboard box, making *'broom, broom!'* sounds and pushing it around inside the home; and we might well describe this same action with words such as "Jessie is driving the car." However, we would also use the words "Jessie is driving the car" when explaining how a person gets from the airport to their home. Confusing these two scenarios would be nonsense in the physical world.

Likewise, if we are left only with the words, "being awake while asleep," and have never ourselves had an experience of lucid dreaming and a continuity of consciousness in the planes of other consciousnesses, then our intellect may indeed confuse these two extremely different realities, regarding them as the same thing. Not only are they not the same thing, but lucid dreaming leads to the potential danger of being caught in the diverting aspects of the elemental or astral world, whilst continuity of consciousness leads to deep inner strengthening in the spiritual world.

In the physical world, we all know from our experience that our application of words is corrected by the immediate reality of the world around us. Not so regarding descriptions of the spiritual world; here, everything has to be experienced in order to be understood as a living reality. In the spiritual world, our reality is dependent on our ability to experience it. Often, with spiritual content it is not a matter of *what* is said, but of the experience of the reality *behind* what is said, which is being *pointed to* with the words.

If you have never had the direct experience yourself, or the ability to contemplate the content of esoteric work with the depths of your thinking, then a thousand confusions could arise in a person's notion of the true developmental path. It can be very difficult to differentiate a true understanding, arising from a *rightly conceived* developmental path, of what is yet to be experienced on this path, from an understanding based mainly on our intellectual prejudices.

This holds true for the numerous experiences that the student of the work must encounter. So often we imagine that we have lost the way, when in fact the experience in question is a necessity of the path. Our intellect is expecting certain things that we have read about, but these have simply been read without a close enough understanding. Because of this, many truths lie concealed even when written in black and white. We often overlook genuine inner changes due to the fact that we are only expecting to encounter what we have read about and understood in a narrow sense with our intellect. All this can delay our onward progress.

In the inner training, some of these confusions are avoided through the inner path being given in terms of meditative exercises, verses, and mantras that cannot be diverted or misunderstood as easily by materialistic thinking. They speak to the deeper soul, and if they are engaged with as they are given, they will produce results that lead the student further.

The meditative exercises, verses, and mantras work upon one in such a way that, regardless of the level of development thus-far attained by the student, the true inner schooling exercises contain within them the training required for the soul to develop the capacities with which to meet different worlds at different levels or grades.

Yet we are even tempted to alter these exercises in order to suit our preferences or our given understanding at a certain time. If we could rightly comprehend the majesty of the inner training, then we would not be tempted to make things up. For this is not our task; our task is to walk the well-trodden path leading to genuine spiritual experience and therefore transformation. The true path has a way, even though we will each walk it uniquely.

One of our great difficulties is finding the language that can serve to relate the wisdom of the esoteric work to our individual experience in walking the path. Even within anthroposophy, the language or terminology has been changed over the years. Various terminologies are used to describe the worlds or planes of consciousness that the human being can traverse through the path of inner development. It seems that it is of greater use to rely on our experience rather than on terminology, as it is only when the individual's experiences are evaluated alongside the great teachings that we truly come to know and understand these worlds.

Understanding the complexity of the human being, as well as the levels or planes of consciousness that we are able to experience, is the enquiry and investigation of the spiritual scientist. In the body of work known as anthroposophy, Rudolf Steiner has given hundreds of lectures from his direct research into the spiritual worlds. Yet his call to those who are drawn to the inner work is: *I do not want you to believe me, but to understand me.*[7] Many individuals have now embarked on this great journey of understanding these realms of consciousness and the quality of the consciousnesses that reside there.

In order to understand our place in the developmental process of the physical world, we need to gain insight into what makes up the human being from an esoteric point of view.

In the light of anthroposophy, the human being, as it stands in the sense world, is comprised of four bodily sheaths. The spirit and soul unite with, and utilize, these bodily sheaths in order for the human being to participate in earthly life. The physical body allows us to participate in the world around us, experiencing the external, sense-perceptible world through our own sensory vehicle. It provides us with the vehicle with which we are able to be a human being in a definite place and space. The etheric- or life-body provides the living, growing element; it is the vehicle by means of which the human being is able to grow through time and the unfolding of life-processes. The astral body is the direct vehicle for soul activity, and the ego sheath is the vehicle for the spirit's direct expression.

All the traditions of the spirit agree that the true essence of the human being is the eternal spirit. In several traditions, it is expressed as the 'I am,' which is present from one incarnation to the next. Although the 'true I' continues to reside in the spiritual world and only has its *reflection* in the ego-sheath or 'sheath-I' in the physical world, the 'higher I' is the individual spiritual consciousness expressed within each individual being.

Each individual human being also has capacities of soul. The soul capacities work through the astral body as they come to expression in the physical world. The human soul is beyond nation, race, tribe, religion, gender, and sex. The soul, in-itself, is neither male nor female. It is neither black nor white, nor any other skin color or race. It is not American, British, or Chinese, nor does it belong to any outer land or country. These things are the aspects that, in this life, your soul is experiencing—and yet, in another life the same soul will be experiencing different things.

The 'I' and the soul-capacities together constitute our greater self. Even though we tend to think that the body together with the particular personality and life-circumstances is the self, in the reality of the spirit the true self consists of all that is not transient but *eternal*; it consists of the eternal nature of our 'I'-being and soul capacities.

However, we need the vehicle of the body in order to experience our individual life. How would we come to know who we are and why we are here if we did not incarnate into a separate bodily vehicle? How would we continue the aspects of evolution that can only take place through life on earth?

The bodily vehicle allows us to ask these questions. Without the experience of being a separated individual 'I'-consciousness, we would not be able to ask the question, *Who am I?* And yet, because of this same bodily vehicle, we can lose sight of who we truly are and why we are here. In lectures to the Waldorf teachers, Rudolf Steiner said that the first prerequisite of the Waldorf teacher is to have reverence for the soul-spiritual potential that the child is bringing into the world. What is the nature of the soul-spiritual potential dwelling in this other being? In the Child Study, we spend more time looking at the bodily sheaths than we do attempting to perceive the soul-spiritual being. It can be helpful to asses the vehicle, because once we recognize what belongs to the outer vehicle, we can then put this to one side in order to discern what belongs to the spiritual being with its soul capacities, which is beyond the vehicle. When all that is transient is put to one side, we are left with the eternal. We can ask the question, *What is left of me after everything of a transient nature is removed?*

In relation to the physical body, we have to remove the polarities of being male or female, and of the constitutional tendency to nerve-sense-system- or metabolic-system-dominance. In the etheric body, we remove the temperaments and the cultural conditioning, including that of gender and social standing. We remove race, religion, and family beliefs. In the astral body we remove the planetary qualities that affect our character and all our biographical patterns. When we take all this away—when we remove all that belongs to this transient self—then the eternal remains.

Building the relationship to the eternal is achieved through building a relationship to the inner eternal worlds, to the spiritual world. Building this relationship is the path of inner work.

Within the instrument of the astral body, the soul expresses soul-capacities; the soul utilizes the astral body as its direct vehicle through thinking, feeling, and willing. But in the sense world, the etheric and physical bodies place the soul in certain circumstances and situations, in time and space, within which we apply our thinking, feeling, and will.

The ego is the sheath of *spiritual activity*: the expression of the *individual spiritual will* as opposed to the will-activity of the *soul*. The spirit utilizes the ego-sheath in order to express its individual being. The spirit, through the astral body, gathers experience; through the etheric body, it is placed in time and experiences growth; and through the physical body, it is placed in space. These four sheaths interpenetrate one another in everyday life. In each sheath we can find the traces of the other components at work. Through the various forces that hold sway in the four sheaths, the human personality arises.

In the sense world, it is the physical sheaths that dominate. My life-body is bound to my physical experience. Therefore in the sense world, the astral body with its thinking, feeling, and willing is bound to the sense experiences, and the same is true of the ego. I know myself to be an 'I' in the world of sense because the body gives me that boundary between self and other. In the physical, sense-perceptible world, the laws of the physical dominate. And what I carry within me as the other members of my being, originating from other worlds, falls into the background and slumbers in comparison to the strength of sense-perceptible experiences.

A kind of anesthetization of the higher members takes place through the sense world's dominating might. This influence seems to be ever-increasing as the materialistic age progresses; as a result, it becomes harder for individuals to naturally know and feel that a higher life exists. Today we must work consciously towards this knowledge.

The whole of the period since the middle of the 19th century has been one of anesthetization through the impressions received by the senses. It is the great illusion of this age that the overly powerful life of the senses has been considered to be the right one—that life of the senses whose aim was to obliterate completely the life in the cosmos beyond the earth.[8]

In order to begin to understand the primary task of our development in the sense world, and to understand the experiences of the soul-spiritual life in other realms of being, we need to evaluate our experiences in the physical world and to recognize the interplay of the various aspects of our human nature.

In the physical world, the four members of the human being are at work in a particular way; this differs from the way in which they are at work in the elemental world, and again from how this is so in the lower spiritual world and the higher spiritual world. As we raise ourselves into higher worlds, the lower members are left behind. It is only in the physical world that we see all four members of the human being interpenetrating one another.

The physical body is a vehicle for the human being in space; through this physical body, the other members of the human being come into relationship with the outer world. The *etheric body*, or *life-body*, is subdued through the way in which it is bound to the body of the physical-sense world. Its experience of vitality, health, and wellbeing is dependent on the condition of the metabolic system. The life-body is the foundation of the capacity to feel and experience movements within the rhythmic system, and it is the limited substance through which thinking can be carried out and reflected via the nerve-sense system.

The *soul-body*, with the capacities of thinking, feeling, and will, is also chained to the sense-experiences of the physical world through the astral body.

The *sentient soul* is directly bound to the astral sheath, the *intellectual soul* to the etheric body, and the *consciousness soul* to the physical body. During the course of human evolution, the soul has been taken hold of in a way that allows us a certain freedom in how this 'boundness' comes to expression.

The whole of humanity has a role to play in the collective development of the human race. Through the working of the ego upon the soul over time, it has allowed us varying degrees of independence from the physical sheath. The sentient soul has been worked upon in the sentient-soul age, which lasted from around 3000 BC until 747 BC; during the course of this time-period, it was liberated from its binding to the astral sheath.

The fact that we, as human beings today, do not need to follow the longings and cravings of the connection between our astral body and sentient soul, is due to the previous workings of humanity; before this time, the sentient soul sought pleasure and avoided pain in an instinctive way, almost as can be seen in the animal kingdom. For the human being to have evolved past that kind of inner dominance and un-freedom, in which we were not the masters of our own inner life of desires, it was necessary for the collective human development to grow onwards in the sense of the sentient soul's liberation.

The human beings of times past took hold of this instinctual connection and gradually liberated it over time.

In order to achieve this, certain forms were introduced, such as the practice of imposed will over other human beings (i.e., that of the ancient Egyptian Pharaoh over the general populace). This practice served to force the 'instinctual self' to work on behalf of the greater good. Looking back to ancient Egypt, the use of enslavement as a way of ordering society takes on a different meaning when seen in this light. In this sense, it was a training that was necessary in order to enable the human soul to cultivate the new faculties of those times. Any thought of such forms of enslavement is abhorrent to us now, and so it should be, for now it would not be a valid part of human development. In fact, all such forms of enslavement from 747 BC onwards could only have been, and could only be, a means of degrading the human being below its potential.

Development of the sentient soul has taken place through the work of collective humanity; whether we make use of this development or not, it is there for all human beings who now walk the earth. As a result of this development, we are now in a position where we may choose to follow our instincts and cravings, or not to follow them. This inner freedom is in each of our hands because of the work of others to evolve from the state of leading life according to animalistic impulses, to that of the emergence of new reasoning faculties capable of responding and relating to life by other means.

The *intellectual soul* has been worked upon and taken hold of from 747 BC until 1413 AD. The age of the intellectual soul in ancient Greece brought with it philosophy and didactics. Developing thinking and the reasoning mind was one of the great tasks of the intellectual-soul age. In order to think through life decisions, the portion of humanity then at work needed to liberate the intellectual soul from its overly bound relationship to the etheric body. Prior to this age, intellectual thinking was not a primary and universal faculty among human beings. The reason we are now able to rationally think through matters that present themselves in our lives is due to the collective evolution of human beings living at this earlier time.

Instead of living out of 'hand-me-down' beliefs from the past, we are now able to make reasoned decisions on the basis of thinking through why we do what we do. We can also think in a scientific way that allows us to understand the world of the past, and on that basis to conceive of how we should rightly progress into the future. With the reasoning mind, sometimes the decisions we arrive at can even go against personal pleasure, enabling us to live out of higher ideals. With the intellectual-soul age came laws that determine how we should live together according to the collective thought processes. Religious scholars were consulted. The scholars of thought established and directed the social forms. The establishment of 'codes of conduct' on the basis of religion, culture, family, and tribe had a place in determining the thoughts of the collective social life and structures.

The divisions of peoples in terms of culture, religion, social standing, and gender roles had a place in organizing the structure of society in the past. Today we would see such forms as digressive to human progress, even though at one point in our evolution they may have been deemed necessary for our development as laws of conduct enforced onto the various groups. Now, in the *consciousness-soul* age, it is our responsibility to combat things which had a place then, but do not now.

> Other qualities which, like anger and vexation, have to be combated are timidity, superstition, prejudice, vanity and ambition, curiosity, the mania for imparting information, and the making of distinctions in human beings according to the outward characteristics of rank, sex, race, and so forth. In our time it is difficult for people to understand how the combating of such qualities can have anything to do with the heightening of the faculty of cognition. But every spiritual scientist knows that much more depends on such matters than upon the increase of intelligence and the employment of artificial exercises.[9]

Today we have laws that prevent discrimination towards race, gender, and religion because we are becoming aware of the rights of the individual. This is a mark of the consciousness-soul age. Martin Luther King was a human being developing the liberation of the consciousness-soul; he famously stated that *human beings should not be judged by the color of their skin, but by the content of their character.*[10] As this age progresses, we will be able to live this truth as well as many other developments that will come about in the course of the consciousness-soul age; but it is up to humanity now to carry out this work of liberation. We are only at the beginning of this age.

The more we learn to judge people according to their inner faculties, to deepen life inwardly, the more we help to bring about what must be the basic character of a future humanity.[11]

Since the 15th century, we have entered into the consciousness-soul age; the human beings of this age have a task. We are now to liberate the consciousness soul from its state of being bound to the physical body. The physical body, which has given us a separate sense of self, continues to inform the consciousness soul. The great gift of the consciousness-soul age is the growing awareness of our individuality. We are able to have independent thoughts, feelings, and will-impulses that do not stem from gender, family, race, and so forth.

However, the great difficulty will be to continue to live and work together as members of the whole human society. The deep sense of isolation that arises as the consciousness soul awakens can be overwhelming to some people. We are developing a new capacity that allows us to live and respond to life not out of instincts or the sentient soul, nor out of the reasoning mind or the intellectual soul, but out of a place of knowing and recognition of what is needed. The ego—the bearer of the individual spiritual will—most clearly lights up and becomes perceptible in the consciousness soul.

All human beings of our time recognize that there is an external self and an internal self. As our biographical lives develop, we exteriorize our internal self towards the external self. What we think and feel and do is increasingly called forth by the external world and who we are within it. But we may also close the door to the external world and descend consciously into our inner being, into our inner life. Our everyday thinking, which is bound to the external world, can be discovered in a new way in our inner life. Usually we think about all the things we need to do in the outer world, the people we need to see, the interactions we need to have. Alternatively, instead of focusing all our attention on these outer things, we can also think about questions of a different nature—inner questions, such as: *What is life all about? Why do I do what I do? What are the forces that compel me in one direction or another? How can I look at my own thinking and evaluate it?*

The inner world presents very different questions from those presented by the outer world of the senses. In the inner world, we begin to recognize the difference between the 'me'-self—the everyday self—and the 'I am' consciousness. We first become capable of awakening to this 'I am' consciousness *in our inner world*. Some might call this 'I am' consciousness 'the witness' or 'the observer.' In order to have a capacity to witness my thoughts, my feelings, and my behaviors, part of my being must maintain an existence independent of, separate from, the externalizing of all my forces towards the outer world. In order to witness, we must maintain an inner awareness.

In order to more clearly perceive the sentient, intellectual, and consciousness-soul forces at work within ourselves today, we can try a few inner exercises that give us a sense for the quality of these three soul forces.

1) *From sentient soul to intellectual soul*

Think of something that you desire to do; it can be something very small, like the desire to eat a particular food—or it can be something very large, like the desire to pursue a particular relationship. Holding the desire in your mind, now think of all the reasons not to do what you desire. Think of all the negative or unproductive aspects involved in what you desire to do. Produce a list of *cons* that helps you to evaluate it from this different perspective.

What is the quality experienced in the desire body, the sentient soul? What happens when the rational thinking comes in, bringing all the reasons you should not do what you desire?

For many, there is a sense of restriction, of being deflated, of being contained and held back; sometimes guilt or similar feelings arise when bringing out all the reasons against, all the *cons* to doing what you desire.

It is interesting to note that, on one hand, our sentient soul often feels like the younger part of us; and on the other hand, it feels like the part that gives us passion and vitality for life and for the things we want to do.

2) *From intellectual soul to consciousness soul* [12]

Imagine a circle divided into three equal parts. Now remove the circle and you are left with a 'Y'-shaped form. On the left arm of the 'Y', the phrase 'command me' is written. On the right arm of the 'Y', the phrase 'forbid me' is written (all this is done imagined in the mind's eye; not on paper). On the center arm, there are no words.

Now think of a decision that you have to make; it can be a small decision or a large decision. Once you have thought of the decision in your mind, then, along the left arm of the 'Y', you think through in logical order everything positive that could result from saying 'yes' to the decision. Even though you surely can't think of *every* possible outcome, you can still think through as many positive possibilities as you can imagine. In this way, you can empty your intellectual soul of all the thoughts it might have regarding the positive reasons to make this decision.

Then, on the right arm, where the phrase 'forbid me' has been written, you think through again in logical sequence all the possible negative outcomes to saying 'yes' to this decision. Once you have thus exhausted the intellectual soul, the reasoning mind, on the two arms of the 'Y', then you ignore the two arms of the 'Y' and simply concentrate or focus your attention on the center line.

While focusing your attention on the center line, do not look for an answer as to which path to choose; do not look for a 'yes I should,' or 'no I shouldn't.' Rather, seek the quality of the center line. The quality of the liberated consciousness-soul expresses itself as a sense of knowing or presence of being, of feeling centered in yourself.

This exercise begins to reveal the quality of the consciousness soul. The liberated consciousness soul, or what Rudolf Steiner sometimes referred to as the "spiritual soul," is our link to the spirit.[13] The spirit neither commands nor forbids us. Many people experience the 'inner center' as a quality of centeredness or peace. Some experience it as an 'iron rod' of knowing, whereas others experience it as calmness, surety, or inner recognition of the truth.

Through this exercise, you can begin to recognize the difference between the inner activity that comes into effect when the intellectual soul is operating, as compared to that which can be felt when the consciousness soul is working in our lives.

This new faculty, which is gradually developing in the consciousness-soul age, gives us the capacity to *recognize* what is right for us to do, instead of intellectualizing and trying to work out what we *'need'* to do. This capacity is becoming ever more essential in our times: the ability to know what is ours to do.

In our times, this seems more relevant than ever before, considering all the information available, and all the intellectual studies that are being carried out. We are sometimes left with no other choice but to find another way beyond the intellectual acrobatics we are prone to as a result of the decisions we need to make. For instance, the research available on something like 'hormone replacement therapy' (HRT) reveals to us completely contradictory information. Two of the most highly regarded university research teams battle in opposition to each other with regard to the use of HRT. One university has accumulated detailed research supporting the notion that women should be on HRT, that this is an absolute necessity for the physical health of the body—also, that it helps to prevent certain cancers, the loss of bone density, etc. Another research team arrives at a completely opposite conclusion. It states that HRT should only be used when absolutely necessary: when the symptoms of menopause are so extreme that the risks are outweighed by its ability to decrease severe menopausal symptoms. They say that this kind of intervention should be used for a limited period of time only. This work asserts, on the basis of scientific research, that HRT causes the increase of cancers and that in most cases the risks far outweigh the potential benefits.

The situation of 'oppositional scientific research'—where two or more prominent schools, both based on scientific research, come to opposite viewpoints—is becoming increasingly common. Science-based research does not have all the answers, especially where we see studies that will potentially result in financial gain for pharmaceutical companies or other interested parties. It is a well-documented fact that the question of how to give healthy people medications they don't need is an area of research that pharmaceutical companies are investing in. There is greater financial gain to be made in putting more people on pharmaceuticals than there is in prescribing them only to the people who need them. The decision to 'lower the mark' of what is considered an acceptable, healthy blood-pressure level was made during the last decade by several people with vested interests in pharmaceutical companies. We cannot find our way through life by means of other people's opinions, nor even through so-called 'evidence-based' science. Therefore, we cannot exclusively use the intellectual soul in our decision-making processes. Especially with the most important things in life, we need to do what we *know* is right—not merely what we are *told* to do.

Let us take as an example something far less important, such as staying at a hotel. Going to *Trip Advisor* and finding other people's opinions may sway us, but often the people commenting on the hotel contradict each other. One person says, "It's the cleanest, nicest, friendliest place I've ever stayed at." Another says, "It is the dirtiest, most unfriendly hotel I have ever stayed at." In such a situation, trying to follow the reasoning mind—the mind that works things out by weighing the so-called facts—no longer works for us. We have to seek another capacity to steer us through all the options of life.

When it comes to important decisions, only the highest element in us can make the right choice. Esoterically, even the so-called small decisions make a difference to our karmic meetings and encounters. It is said that it makes a difference where you have your coffee in the morning, which cafe you choose to drink it in. It must also be that it makes a difference where we sleep at night; it makes a difference where we are all the time—for where we are changes our destiny, it changes our encounters. It changes the whole event, not only for us, but for others. How do we make these decisions that steer us forward?

The question is: What is it that leads our lives? We always have a choice. We can respond to life's choices from our sentient soul, that part of the soul that seeks pleasure and avoids pain, and is patterned by our biography. Or we can respond to life through our intellectual soul, our reasoning mind, trying to work out what would make the most sense to us. Or, finally, we can respond to life from the consciousness soul, as it gives us the sense of inner recognition, a sense of what is right to do or not to do— of where we need to be or do not need to be.

The consciousness soul or spiritual soul is our most progressive soul-force. Through working with it and developing our relationship to the quality that the consciousness soul brings, we are working with the most progressive elements available to the earthly human being in our times.

In order to work with the spiritual forces that are leading humanity forward, with what are called the "progressive gods," we must be working with the most progressive element in our own being. As a collective humanity, right now the progressive element is the consciousness soul. Although we are just at the beginning of its development, the only way we will succeed in cultivating its capacities is if we are consciously working with what it seeks to bring.

The human being can only become free in the spirit. So long as we are dependent upon the physical nature in which our spirit dwells, we remain its slave. We can become free only when we rediscover ourselves in the spirit, and from out of the spirit, gain mastery over what is within us.[14]

As we can see from what has been outlined above, the primary focus of our earthly consciousness at this stage of human evolution is the *consciousness soul development*. (In my book, *Developing the Self*, all three soul-elements are discussed in relation to the exercises that can be used to take hold of them. The other soul-sheaths first need to be worked through in order that the consciousness soul does not work in service of one's particular, merely personal preferences.)

Developing the consciousness soul requires three faculties or capacities that the student must work to develop. One of these capacities is *presence of mind*; for many, this is the first step in their consciousness-soul development. Many individuals have come to recognize that they need this sense of presence, or what in some Eastern traditions is called *mindfulness*. Some have called this step "developing the witness." The 'witness'-self is the part of us that is able to look upon our sentient-soul reactions, and can even observe our intellectual-soul trying to work things out—yet recognizes itself as something other, something more than, these soul-components. It is able to observe them at work, trying to lead our lives in certain directions.

However, we need to be cautious not to develop this aspect to the exclusion of the other aspects; as the hermetic saying goes, *Watch the watcher, examine the examiner, judge the judge*. That is to say, mindfulness, or this 'witness,' is only *one* step. And it is one that, in-and-of-itself, could potentially bring the human being towards greater isolation and egotism—especially if the individual develops mindfulness in relation to their inner life and soul-responses *only* in order to gain an advantage for their personal 'me'-self in the physical, sense world. This would signify that the consciousness soul is being utilized by the less progressive soul elements.

Mindfulness practices are often promoted as tools for sensory gratification and gain, such as the goal of becoming the best CEO in order to gain more for your shareholders. Notions such as this are being promoted worldwide on the basis of certain techniques of inner development. Such notions have even been declared openly as a valid motivation for undertaking one's own development, so that, as one speaker on meditation promoted, "in your next life you can get yourself a Fifth Avenue womb." In this way human beings misuse the potential development of collective humanity, and apply it instead for their own personal gain. For example, it is common that people use the expression 'this is my truth,' when in fact the opinion in question has nothing to do with the truth, but only expresses the desire to gratify a personal preference.

True presence will be mindful of the desire to comfort oneself and of inner greed, mindful of the desire for self-service; true mindfulness will not be used in order to ensure that the self is served. This will be brought to clarity once we include the other aspects of consciousness-soul development.

Another necessary aspect of this development is *reverence*; reverence is needed in order to gain access to something beyond ourselves. As we enter more deeply into this consciousness-soul age, we will need to develop an individual relationship to the guiding support of the consciousnesses that help humanity. To think that we are the 'be all and end all' of the consciousness at work in the cosmos is a form of pride that would lead us to severe paths of egotism—forms of egotism even greater than we have seen influence humanity thus far. The consciousness-soul age could lead our attention away from anything higher existing outside of the 'me'-self, due to the body-bound nature of this soul-force. The schooling of the consciousness-soul leads the student to surrender the personal self to the *spiritual* or *greater self*.

There are four steps to this surrender; the first is *wonder*. Wonder allows us to open ourselves to the possibility of something else—something we do not already know. We open ourselves to something that exists beyond what is already known to us. This gesture contains a quality of *awe*, particularly when we look to the wonders of nature.

Step two, already mentioned above, is *reverence*. From wonder, we move to reverence. There is a difference, inwardly, when we practice openness towards something, or when we revere something. The quality of reverence presupposes that what we open to is of a higher nature. As we open in reverence to the world of nature, this leads us naturally to step three, where there is a beginning *recognition of the wisdom-filled harmony* holding

33

sway between what lives in us as individuals, and what lives in the outer cosmos. All the esoteric lessons or knowledge-teachings aim to reveal the deep mystery: "O Humankind, thou art the condensed image of the world! O World, thou art the being of humankind poured out into infinite space!"[15]

The final step, step four, is *surrender*. This is then achievable because we do not surrender to the void of nothingness, to the processes of death, but actually to the processes of rebirth. Contemplating the path from *wonder* to *reverence* to *wisdom-filled harmony* and *surrender*, we recognize the inner schooling that the consciousness soul must take if we are not to shut ourselves up within ourselves during this time in humanity's evolution.

The other capacity of the consciousness soul is *remembering who we are and why we are here*. In this way, we begin to work towards cultivating an awareness of the larger picture of life and our place and task within it. Usually, as we walk through our daily life we forget that we are a spiritual being and that all that unfolds in front of us is a *call to develop*. Through this *remembering*, we are working towards *Imaginative consciousness*: pictorial, living thinking. Imaginative consciousness begins with our ability to think not in an abstract way, separating our thoughts in the intellectual-dissecting manner, but to think in a *unified* context: to begin to think in pictures that place thoughts within the larger world of thoughts. Things are related to each other not because of our ability to rationally order our thoughts, but because they belong to the whole. Our capacity for ordered thinking is only a reflection of the organic unity that holds sway in the world of ideas.

When someone has begun to develop the consciousness soul, they begin to make choices in their life from this inner place. It becomes evident that there is not simply *one* correct way when it comes to facing each decision of the physical world. However, it is only a matter of finding the way that *the particular individual* needs to walk. For one woman, saying 'yes' to HRT is the path she needs to walk. For another, saying 'no' HRT is the path that woman needs to walk. Who guides our life? From what place do we make our decisions? Some people decide not to vaccinate their children, from a point of view that wishes to be fashionable or to be seen as progressive. Others decide not to vaccinate their children because they recognize that this is the path they need to walk. Some people choose to vaccinate their children based on fear, or not wanting to 'rock the boat'—while others choose to vaccinate their children because they recognize it is the right path for them to walk. When someone decides to take a course of antibiotics, we should be more concerned with *what* in them makes that decision than our personal belief of whether it is right or wrong. Is the decision made out of fear, on the basis of an outer authority, or from an individual sense of it being the right path to walk?

The spiritual world is not concerned so much with the outer expression of things, but with *how* we meet life and *from which part* of our being we are directing our lives. *Who and what* we will meet as a result of the decisions we make is more significant. *How* things will unfold, the outcome and the consequences of our lives, will all change depending on our decisions. If we work out of the place in us that seeks for an inner recognition that 'this is the path I need to walk,' then we can also accept that what we meet on the path is exactly what we need to meet. What we will meet is that which will continue to school us. The higher element, which speaks through the consciousness soul, does not lead us down the easiest route. It leads us down the route that will give us what is needed for our next step of development.

> In the fifth post-Atlantean epoch, every single soul has difficulties that they must encounter; for the conscious-ness-soul can develop only through the testing occa-sioned by the overcoming of these difficulties.[16]

As we develop our consciousness-soul activity, we also begin to recognize when it is working in others. We can begin to hear when someone is making decisions in their life out of anxiety, out of beliefs, out of unconsciousness. We can also hear when someone is inwardly clear and recognizes the steps they need to take. We can hear the desires working; we can hear when people are lying, even when they lie and do not know themselves to be lying. We hear the voice of deception speaking. We listen to a news report and know that we are being manipulated, even though the newsreaders themselves do not know that they are voicing propaganda. We can hear when the good is spoken; we can hear the truth in things that we do not yet know through personal trial to be true.

Hafiz expresses this in the poem "Cast All Your Votes for Dancing":

> Whenever you say God's name, dear pilgrim,
> My ears wish my head was missing
> So they could finally kiss each other
> And applaud all your nourishing wisdom![17]

To recognize a given capacity in the other, this capacity must first be developed within ourselves. To hear who is speaking, we must first hear who speaks in us. As the students develop these capacities further, they will begin to be able to detect three voices in every decision: the sentient soul, the intellectual soul, and the consciousness soul. Hearing the various soul-choices does not mean that we will automatically follow the highest voice within us. We are free to choose, but we also come to know which forces are compelling us.

All three of the consciousness-soul capacities, taken together, open up to the progressive, supportive spiritual forces that are assisting humanity in its development forward. They always leave us free; to not leave us free would be going against the progressive beings. If we feel that we have no freedom and no choice, then we should look more closely at what soul-forces are compelling us.

It is through the development of the consciousness soul that we can safely and clearly enter the elemental world. No one can participate with clarity in the elemental world unless the consciousness-soul faculties are engaged. And yet, we are already beginning to cross that threshold. In many cases we are crossing unprepared.

All the inner schooling exercises serve to prepare the human being for steps or stages of consciousness beyond the stage at which the individual currently stands. This is quite an extraordinary mystery pertaining to the exercises given through esoteric training. Regardless of our level of development, they can work upon us, helping us to cultivate the next step. As the hermetic saying goes, *Do not stop on any step, no matter how high, or it will become a snare.* If we take one of the basic esoteric verses, we can begin to see how it helps to train us.

More radiant than the sun,
Purer than the snow,
Finer than the ether
Is the self,
Spirit in my heart.
I am this self,
This self am I.[18]

The verse must first be worked with in accordance with the training. If we look at this verse and spend our time judging it, appraising it, and perhaps giving our own opinions of it, we do not learn anything from the verse; rather, we amplify the 'me'-self. It is 'all about us.' In a certain way, those with a weakened sense of self, a weakened *'sheath-I' sense*, may find that coming into relationship with esoteric verses in this way strengthens their 'sheath-I' sense—in the same way that all life strengthens our earthly-'I' sense if we enter into relationship with the world through making a division between *what it is* and what we *judge it to be.*

However, in order to use this verse esoterically, we need to give ourselves—at least our attention, our presence of mind—for a small period of time each day, and concentrate on the verse we wish to work with.

This helps us to develop *presence*: the ability to draw my attention to something that I choose to be attentive to. In addition, the verse cultivates within us a reverence towards 'the other.' It helps us to raise ourselves to something that is beyond the everyday 'me'-self. All the verses given on the path of esoteric schooling help us to cultivate a reverence for 'the beyond.' At the same time, we are working towards 'remembering the truth' through the pictures of these imaginations. This is not an intellectual dissecting of 'what constitutes the true self,' but rather an image that is pointing, suggesting, and developing a picture within ourselves. These verses work in us as a means of helping us to connect with the greater world.

Esoteric schooling provides us with what we need in order to cultivate the next step in our development, if only we give it our time, energy, and attention. Even if the time we give to the esoteric verse is spent judging it and forming opinions about it, this will nevertheless help us eventually, albeit slowly, to reach the next step. However, if we work with the verse rightly, then we can begin to work towards cultivating not only a stronger sense of *personal self*, but we can also begin to develop the consciousness-soul capacities leading *beyond* the personal self. Those who have begun to develop these consciousness-soul capacities will, through working with the same given verse, begin to develop the capacities required for consciously experiencing the elemental world.

Our outer, material world is made up of physical substance; we can see it, we can weigh it, and we can evaluate it. In contrast, the elemental world is made up of what might be called 'thought substance.' Thought is an *activity of consciousness* when it is not bound to the world of the senses, but is rather working as an independent force within the self. When walking through the sense world, we encounter the other beings belonging to this world. As we walk through the elemental world, we meet the substance of the thoughts of other beings. It is not a world that exists 'somewhere *other*' than the realm of consciousness. It can only be experienced through our inner life. It is not touched by the physical senses, but is touched through the 'inner senses.' It is a world of experience imperceptible to the senses. Those who experience this realm know such experiences to be not only *as real* as the external world, but *more real* than the external world. Understanding this world is a necessity in understanding the multitude of experiences that a person aspiring on the path of inner development will need to encounter, and beyond which they will need to grow.

The ego or 'sheath-I' recognizes itself as an 'I'-being through the current connection to the individual separate bodily form provided by the physical sheath. As the human being passes from the sense world into the elemental world, it leaves behind the physical sheath that had previously dampened down the experience of the other members of our being.

Upon releasing itself from the body-bound nature, the human being immediately enters the world of living thought-processes: the elemental world. It is the new world in which the soul, together with the 'I', finds itself. Up until the point at which the soul-spirit element is loosened from the physical world, the *elemental world* —through its inherent relationship to the etheric body— had played a role in allowing the thoughts within us to take shape. This is because in the substance of thinking, the elemental world is already working, though to a very subdued degree. *'Living thinking'* is achieved through rising into the elemental world.

Thoughts that are no longer attached to, and developed out of, the external world *live in this elemental world.* The elemental world is where the thoughts of human beings become alive—in a world that now appears to be outside our consciousness. Thoughts experienced in the elemental world seem to be *more real* than the thoughts experienced in the physical world. The dull thought-life of the grey, intellectual thoughts born of the physical world is now transformed in the elemental world. Not only do our thoughts become living, but we can *experience* them. In this living substance of the elemental world, the human soul is alive in a completely new way.

Rudolf Steiner has stated that thinking lives in the etheric. In the area of our head, the etheric element is already loosened slightly, which is what grants us the capacity we do have for thinking in the sense world. To understand this, try this brief exercise. Close your eyes and imagine an object. Try to picture, with your thinking forces, a pencil. Where do you see the pencil? For most people it is just in front of the forehead. It is not pictured inside the physical space of the head, but in the surrounding space. Now call up inwardly a feeling, such as the feeling of joy. This feeling is initially experienced within the boundaries of our human body; and then it is possible for the experience to extend beyond the body. Now try moving your hand; you can see how the will-forces are tied to the physical body. In the elemental world, as the etheric element loosens to a far greater degree, this capacity for thinking is increased tenfold and the quality of thinking changes.

In order to enter the elemental world, the etheric first of all loosens in the area around the head to a far greater extent than in normal, daily life. In our inner contemplations, we begin to recognize that 'something else thinks with me'—that thoughts greater than I myself could conjure up are now participating in my thinking, and I am learning from these thoughts.

The human being must find the strength to fill their world of ideas with light and to experience it as light-permeated, even when this experience is unsupported by the anesthetizing world of sense. In this experience of the independent world of ideas—which, in its independence, is permeated with light—the human being's sense of community with the extra-earthly cosmos will reawaken.[19]

Through their own will, the candidate of inner development can strengthen the capacity to receive perceptions of these other worlds. The elemental world is a world of living activity; here thoughts are not dead, formed concepts, but rather living pictures. In time, the etheric element also loosens from the rhythmic system and eventually the metabolic system, each producing extraordinarily enlivening effects on our inner world.

Walking this path of development leads from the sense world, through the elemental world, to the spiritual world. We cannot develop the organs of spiritual perception in the physical world alone. It is only through the time spent by the soul *in the spiritual world* that the organs of spiritual perception can be created. On the meditative path, we are given the form that allows us to enter into those realms in which the organs of perception may then be cultivated.

Our capacity to know and experience on different levels depends on the faculties that we have developed. However, each faculty must be fully developed in the realm to which it corresponds. The saying, *The eye was created by the light for the light*, holds true for all organs of perception.

Without any inner development, we would be oblivious to the working of other realms of consciousness. Through engaging in the path of inner development, we are no longer oblivious; however, for as long as we have not yet developed the organs enabling higher perception, we must first endure the experiences of the other realms with our senses still chained to physical perception alone.

Once we begin to develop these higher capacities, we progress from 'enduring' to the ability to 'sense' the other worlds. Eventually faculties of 'seeing' are cultivated. The organs that give us the capacity to see in worlds imperceptible to the senses enable us to consciously participate in those worlds to which we were once oblivious. We begin to be aroused from the anesthetized slumber, we begin to awaken.[20]

2

INNER DEVELOPMENT FOR THE
ELEMENTAL WORLD

There are several experiences that commonly occur when encountering the other realms of consciousness, although not everyone will experience all of them. They will be expressed here primarily from the point of view of the one undergoing the inner training, who is consciously working with the path of inner development.

There are *three possible modes of experiencing* on this path. There are those who *'see,'* who have awoken their faculties of spiritual sight (this can happen at different stages of the training: for some it is at the beginning; for others, not until the last step). There are those who *'sense'* the spiritual world (we always sense each step before we see it, even if we are 'seers'). These students of the path can recognize that something else is at work in them in addition to their everyday consciousness, and through the esoteric lessons they can evaluate where they are on the path. And then there are those who are experiencing the effects of the training, but are not able to discern from where these effects are arising; therefore, such students often assume that this is just a matter of their 'everyday self' undergoing difficulties. (This same issue likewise presents a challenge for the 'seers' and the 'sensors.') Those in this third group are the students who have to *'endure'* the path until the way becomes clearer through the awakening of certain faculties.

Unlike in our outer biography, in the inner biography an individual may be in the midst of several stages of development simultaneously. One could have crystal-clear insight about certain things, and yet only be capable of sensing others, whilst in the middle of having to endure other steps, all at the same time.

We must also be aware that, in distinction to the crossing that can take place through the path of inner work, there are two further ways of crossing the threshold in our time. There are those who cross the threshold through imbalances arising from employing 'gate crashing' techniques, or through being thrown into imbalance due to illness, accident, or chemical toxicity (the so-called recreational drug user). This kind of crossing produces effects very different from those produced by the trainee of the true path, even if the one speaking of their experiences may use words or descriptions that sound similar to what is found on the true path.

Then there is an increasingly prevalent phenomenon that constitutes the third expression of crossing the threshold into the elemental world in our time. The threshold is naturally being drawn closer to the collective human consciousness, which has given rise to the fact that the experience of other realms is becoming a common phenomenon in our time. The signs that we are witnessing today are of a collective change in inner sensitivity and instability; this change is particularly visible in the younger generations. The effects of this increasingly common kind of crossing, and the ability to manage these effects, are dependent on the previous development the individual who is being drawn across.

The elemental world is the first world that we encounter outside the physical-sense world. In some esoteric schools it is named the "astral world," and Rudolf Steiner used both of these terms. Both terms make sense, for it is home to both the elemental beings and the collective consciousness of the animal kingdom. If the physical world would be represented as the earth, then the elemental world could be the earth's atmosphere.

It is not defined in the same way as a 'spiritual world,' as it has more in common with our earthly experiences than it does with the realities of the spiritual world. The things that we see and experience in the elemental world are not the same as in the physical world, yet certain aspects of their manner of presentation are similar to physical appearances. For example, in the elemental world, we may see shapes, objects, animals, or faces—and the fact that we can use these words to describe what we are seeing indicates a relationship to the physical world. We cannot use such analogous terms in the lower or higher spiritual worlds.

There are certain characteristics of the elemental world that will help us to orient ourselves and to recognize the nature of our elemental experiences. The first of these characteristics is the condition of constant movement and change, or metamorphosis. In the physical world, when we look around us, the fireplace remains a fireplace, the chair remains a chair; whatever we may think of the chair, our thought has no perceptible effect on the way the chair's activity appears to us. The elemental world is a world of living thought-substance. In accord with the laws of the living substance of the elemental world, this world is *affected* by what lives in us; and at the same time, it carries its own laws of growth: it is in a state of constant movement and metamorphosis.

Another characteristic of the elemental world is that it functions according to laws different from those of the physical world. In the physical world, I am here and you are there. In the physical world, there is me, myself—and also that which is outside of me, external to me. This is one of the first differences that the soul must adjust to in the elemental world. There is consciousness of self, and also of my inner world, but my inner world is now *at the same time* outside myself. What once lived as an internal activity of my thoughts and feelings, now presents itself as an external picture moving towards me—and yet, at the same time I still have an internal experience.

Imagine that you sit in front of the mirror and are feeling angry, you pull angry faces: you can see the image of yourself pulling the angry face, and at the same time you are inwardly experiencing the anger. In the elemental world this is a reality; what is thought is now seen, while at the same time it is experienced with far greater intensity. Imagine you have a thought that is cold and calculated. In the elemental world, the thought takes on the form of an image that represents the cold, calculated contours of the thought activity—let's say an 'anvil-like' form. You now see this thought outside of you in the atmosphere, coming towards you as an object, changing in front of you; at the same time, you are having an amplified experience of the quality of this cold, calculated thought within you. The thoughts that live in me are now seen outside me, reflected in the mirror-substance of the elemental world.

It is one of the first, necessary experiences of the elemental world, that in this realm we meet what we ourselves have thought and felt. The thoughts and feelings that in everyday life had streamed forth from us into the outer world, now come back towards us.

This 'mirroring' also comes to expression in *how* we see things. Just as with a mirror, in the elemental world things appear reversed—things are seen 'back to front.' This 'reversing' also comes to expression in the sense that what happened first is seen last. The 'review of the day' exercise is a great preparation for encountering the elemental world. Each night, we go through our day in reverse order. Carrying out this review in *pictures* has the intended effect. Each night, when we leave the body in order to sleep, we pass through the elemental world unconsciously; by carrying out the 'review of the day,' we prepare the way for our experience of this world through preparing the soul to meet it.

There is an Eastern proverb which says that it is easier to catch an arrow flying towards you from someone else's bow than it is to catch the arrow that has left your own bow. In the elemental world, the reverse of this is revealed. Upon initial entry into the elemental world, we encounter the inner world of our own thinking and feeling.

For those who have gained 'inner sight,' the elemental substance presents their thoughts and feelings back to them as pictures. For those who have developed the faculty of 'sensing,' this fact will come to expression as an experience of being bombarded with thoughts and feelings. For those who still do not yet 'sense' it, they will experience their own thinking and feeling as intensifying and perhaps as being less under their own control; they have to 'endure' the initial entry into this world.

This experience of the thought-life intensifying, as one of the first common experiences of the inner apprentice, may be misinterpreted as a 'wrong turn.' Instead of finding the peace and tranquility we may have expected to achieve through inner practice, here we experience thoughts continually bombarding our attempts at meditative practice. Because of the collective 'drawing close' of this threshold, many may experience this difficulty not only in the context of meditative practice itself, but it may also show its effects in daily life as the soul feels more bombarded in this way.

This is a step towards the spirit through the elemental world; through this step, it is common that initially the life of thought does not quiet down, but intensifies. As each step opens up, the student gains more experiences; whether it is a matter of our 'seeing,' 'sensing,' or 'enduring' the inner effects, we gradually come to know what has lived in us. Thankfully, for those undergoing inner training, this generally happens not all at once but in stages.

When we have begun to open up to the constantly changing thought activity of the elemental world, we come to recognize that our inner life requires our stricter governance. If we do not know this, we naturally become influenced by the inner changes and connect these newly intensified thoughts with our everyday sense-world experiences. We may find ourselves thinking about all manner of concerns and considerations, thus feeling ourselves pulled away from meditative activity and more deeply caught up in the external happenings. This battle between my intention to govern my thinking, and the onslaught of thought-activity streaming out from the fact of my having entered into the elemental world, is a necessity. It demands of us that we increase the strength of the ego. Therefore, an intensification of the inner exercises is necessary in order for the ego to establish firmer control over our soul capacities, and thereby regulate our inner life.

A similar reversing occurs with our feeling life. What you have felt inwardly in relation to the world or another person now streams towards you, in a picture form of that feeling. Therefore, we learn to regard in all earnestness the esoteric truth that it is just as harmful to hate another human being, as it is to strike him. Upon entering into the elemental world, many students initially find themselves in an atmosphere of their own making. Students of the inner work come to recognize that their thoughts and feelings affect the elemental atmosphere. In the elemental world, these thoughts and feelings become living picture-forces.

These difficulties are described by Hafiz in his poem, "Will Beat You Up":

Jealousy
And most all of your sufferings
Are from believing
You know better than God,

Of course
Such a special brand of arrogance as that
Always proves disastrous

And will rip the seams
In your caravan tent,

Then cordially invite in many species
Of mean biting flies and
Strange thoughts—
That will
Beat you
Up.[21]

From this first entry into the elemental world, we can see that the basic techniques of 'mindfulness' or 'witnessing' are not enough. It is not enough to say, "I am aware of my negative thoughts"; it is not enough to be mindful of the anger in my soul towards another. It is not even enough to recognize my thoughts as they wander off, watching them like clouds passing by. It *was* enough, *for the physical existence,* to do these things, and it helped us to develop a degree of presence; but now our work needs to be taken further if we are to gather what is needed for passing through the elemental world.

As participators in the elemental world, we come to perceive the consequences of how we conduct our inner life, and thus awaken to our responsibility for this inner life. It becomes all too clear to the student that the inner life needs to be governed. It would be best if we had already developed the habit of governing the inner life even before entering the elemental world; then the onslaught would not be quite as difficult. However, this is not always the case, and with humanity's premature crossing into this realm, it seems that many are forced to endure its effects unprepared.

Just as my actions affect the outer physical world, so does my inner life have an impact on the collective atmosphere of the elemental world. Not only do we encounter our own soul, but we also encounter the collective thought-processes of humanity as a whole. These thoughts present themselves as beings, which rise up before us in the elemental world. They are experienced as *fear, loathing*, and *doubt*. *Fear* of the spiritual world and of what we may encounter there: this fear can block our further work. *Loathing* of what is revealed to us from the spirit can easily turn us away from pressing onwards. And *doubt* in our inner experiences undermines our faith in the path that must be trod. These three beings may show themselves in pictures to the 'seers,' and they send shivers down the spine of the 'sensors'; but all have to 'endure' them at some point. Preparing ourselves for entry into this world will help us to meet them rightly.

In the elemental world—the inner world of myself and others—although this world appears externalized, it is also still a matter of strong *internal* experience. The student now learns and sees and experiences the inner life reflected in the mirror of the elemental life. A cold, calculated thought which I may have had, is now seen and experienced through my own soul life. The elemental world mirrors back to us everything that lives in the human soul. Many first encounters in the elemental world are actually an experience of something in the student's own inner life, which has now become the external life around them. This is why the first stage in inner development is *preparation and purification*: the students of the inner world know that the semblance before them is initially *one of their own making*, and not yet of the *true* spiritual world.

Recently, a school teacher who was trying to work meditatively to understand certain students in his class, recounted that he had been taught to meditate on the first thing that 'popped into his head' about the student. He was taught that the first thing was often the right thing, and that our thinking usually just gets in the way of the right thoughts popping in. His meditation teacher clearly has had no direct experience of the elemental world or the inner life of associations that affect our thinking. When we open ourselves up to meditation, all sorts of nonsense can be 'popping' in that has nothing to do with progression.

In the physical world, our deeds have effects that continue to work upon the environment, until we change these effects; and most often, we can't change what we have carried out in the world as fact. If I cut a rose from the rose bush, that deed means that the environment has been altered. The next person passing the rosebush is not able to see the rose that I have cut and taken with me. If I spill a glass of milk, I can clean it up; yet the fact remains that the milk was spilt, and has a different place in the world than it would have had I drunk the milk. If I were to plant a rose bush and tend to it so that it could grow well, this would also have an effect on the environment.

To the student of the inner work, our inner life becomes a fact that has to be met. When the student of the inner work has awoken to inner sight, they will see their own immoral thoughts streaming towards them as pictures, whilst also experiencing the depth of inner feelings that these thoughts evoke. For the student of the inner work who has not yet awoken to inner sight, they will sense the immoral thoughts bombarding them, assailing them in unseeing warfare. For all others, they will have to endure these returning immoral thoughts as an internal struggle causing inner disturbance. We need to remember that with regard to all the worlds of the spirit, we will first have an inner experience of them before we are able to 'see' them.

Participating in the elemental world through inner training leads the student of the path to develop a necessary feeling of responsibility for their own inner life. In the physical world, we recognize that taking an object from someone, stealing, has an effect: the other loses something and I gain something. In the elemental world, this greed has to be encountered as a primary force that affects the elemental atmosphere now surrounding the student.

Here, there is no 'doing it to the other,' in the sense of how it is in the physical world; in the elemental world, you are 'doing it' to all, including yourself.

The elemental world—as hard as it seems to be to pass through it in full clarity—could also be understood in a helpful sense as *the world of purification and preparation*. As the student awakens to the effects of their own inner life, they begin to experience the necessity of working to strengthen their moral character. These imbalances, if carried further into the higher realm of the spiritual world, will have far greater consequences for the student than they do in the elemental world.

> Whatever is false in thought, whatever is ugly in feeling, and whatever is morally evil, one must oneself erase from existence if it is to be no longer there—and one must do so through the necessary thoughts, feelings, and will impulses or deeds. It will follow one all the time until one has erased it.[22]

In the spiritual world, what you carry with you determines the school that you will enter. If what resonates in the depths of your soul (i.e., not just in the idea you carry about yourself) are the forces of greed and egotism, then these forces will lead you into that schooling which is aimed towards self-gain. At the threshold of the spiritual world, in the purifying elemental world, these things can still be corrected or lose their influence if the inner truth is revealed and seen through the true schooling. This has the effect of leading us past the supportive spiritual Guardian.

In the spiritual world, all the impulses that resonate in the depths of your soul become deeds which assign you to the same beings whose nature it is to perform such deeds. You will be their student and, as such, you will be empowered by inspirations coming from them.

By means of true esoteric lessons and meditative exercises, the meditant is gradually prepared to rightly cross into other realms of consciousness and to encounter greater dimensions of being. The extraordinary thing about the inner schooling path is that one single true exercise can serve to prepare a variety of individuals each standing at a different level of inner training. The first level of training is one of preparation for an encounter with the elemental world.

For this, the ego first needs to be strengthened to a much higher degree than is necessary in the physical world. We need to develop what Rudolf Steiner referred to as the "elemental backbone." The ego can no longer merely rely on the physical boundaries of the body to recognize its own individual nature. Without a heightened capacity of *self-awareness* and *ego strength*, we would lose our consciousness in the vital world of elemental activity. This self-awareness must be developed as an inner 'witnessing' or 'observing' of our own inner life, and not through the sense world doing it for us by giving us the experience of separate boundaries or by confronting us with the outer consequences of our deeds. And the ego's process of inner strengthening can be gained by taking hold of our inner life and thereby cultivating self-mastery. Our heightened ego-capacity is greatly strengthened by our ability to govern and direct our own thinking, feeling, and willing; it is impossible to achieve this heightened strengthening without taking hold of our own soul-forces. In the sense world, our thinking, feeling, and willing are generally drawn forth by the external world around us. Most of the time, we are not the directors of our inner life, but its followers. There is no place for followers on the path of initiation.

At the same time as the ego-capacity is heightened and strengthened, the soul must learn to live within the laws of this new world. This means learning, first of all, *metamorphosis*. Of course, much of what we need to develop can be refined through our experience of the elemental world itself, but if we are not to lose ourselves and our capacities of awareness, then certain strengths in this regard must be developed *before* our entry. On the path of inner training, we are advised to begin the schooling with certain exercises as a preparation for all that will be encountered later.

On the path of inner schooling, preparation for the elemental world is given in various ways. Two of the key preparations for the inner life, learning to enter metamorphosis and learning *picture thinking*, can be achieved in several ways. We are trying to achieve certain capacities, and we must therefore begin to train the soul in ways that will help it adapt to the elemental world. One exercise we could work with is the "metamorphoses of the plant" exercise given in *Knowledge of the Higher Worlds*,[23] where, in your own thinking, you imagine and picture a plant growing out of the seed and all the stages of growth and transformation entailed in this process.

This is an excellent exercise for developing not only the capacity for *picture consciousness*, but also the experience of metamorphosis that we encounter as a matter of course in the elemental world.

By doing the exercises out of our own will-forces, the soul becomes used to, or familiar with, what it will experience in the elemental world. However, we need to do these exercises *with gusto*—we must fill our soul-content as completely as possible with the plant exercise. Our thinking, feeling, and willing must be completely immersed in the exercise for the period of practice. If we notice that we are not able to keep ourselves 'on track' or that some part of our inner life is focused elsewhere, then it is up to us to school ourselves to do the exercise with greater commitment and vigor. This 'pulling' of the soul forces 'onto task' strengthens the ego-capacity considerably.

The verses and mantras given in the esoteric schooling are also a preparation leading to the experience of metamorphosis. However, their usefulness extends far beyond the schooling for the elemental world, as will be shown in the next chapter. But for the sake of differentiating the steps on the path of schooling, I will here describe how to work with these meditations—or rather, how the meditative verse works with the soul—as a preparation for the elemental world.

In approaching meditation exercises involving esoteric verses and mantras, when we unite our soul entirely with each line of the verse, we develop *metamorphosis*. In order to rightly orient itself in the elemental world, the soul needs to become far more flexible and capable of

uniting entirely with the thought or picture of the other.
Let us take the well-known verse:

> More radiant than the sun,
> Purer than the snow,
> Finer than the ether
> Is the self,
> Spirit in my heart.
> I am this self,
> This self am I.[24]

As students of the inner work immerse themselves
with each line, they begin, over time, to develop a certain
flexibility required for the soul-life. *More radiant than
the sun* requires a different quality of 'absorption,' and
produces different effects than does the line *Purer than
the snow*.

Through the inner training, not only are we taught
how to develop the *capacity* needed to enter the various
worlds, but we are also taught *how to meet* these worlds.
In the elemental world, when a picture-thought reveals
itself to our vision, we need to enter fully into the picture.
The soul enters the picture *"More radiant than the
sun"*— then the soul immerses itself in another picture,
"Purer than the snow"—and then into another, and then
another. If in the elemental world we perceive a picture
and remain divided from it, separate from it, then we will
not pass through the elemental world into the spiritual
world. We need to *plunge into* these semblance-pictures
in order to arise into true spiritual activity. Through the

training, we will have learned to unite ourselves with the pictures that arise.

In the elemental world, not all pictures that arise are easy for us to endure, let alone immerse ourselves into. The feelings that we have had towards another, or towards the world, may be experienced as ugly forms when they stream back to us as pictures in the elemental world; the soul naturally recoils from them. Our own thoughts and feelings prevent us from moving through the elemental world, so long as we are unable to unite with the uncomfortable pictures streaming towards us.

In the old Mystery Schools, the hierophant would dress in ugly, grotesque masks in order to train the student to maintain inner equanimity whilst encountering deeply disturbing inner feelings. This preparation is necessary, for in the elemental world not only do we face our own inner life in the course of passing through, but between the beasts and the elemental tricksters we are consistently required to find courage. We must not recoil from the path, but move through, diving into and immersing ourselves in what reveals itself. These esoteric verses teach us *soul flexibility*. These exercises also help us to get used to new laws.

Not only do these exercises help us to achieve all this, but at the same time they serve to enable the soul to carry, *to bear within it*, the wisdom and harmony of the spiritual world, through the truth contained in what is expressed in the lines of the verse. These truths fill our soul with the content that leads to a healthy schooling together with the progressive beings of the spiritual world. Because our soul gradually learns to carry this true content, it will come to resonate with the work and inner nature of the progressive beings.

The inner schooling is not about 'losing ourselves,' but about being able to stand firmly upon the ground in relation to both what is sublime and what is horrifying— and not to recoil, but to enter into it. Without this training, we would not have the soul-flexibility, or the strength and courage, to engage with the elemental world. We would remain on this side of the threshold of the spiritual world. Again, in encountering very uncomfortable experiences in the elemental world, it is necessary to unite with them. We need to be able to 'plunge into' what we are experiencing, in order to go through to the spiritual world. When we encounter an image that creates great fear in us, the soul's natural temptation is to automatically pull back; at that point, we are blocked from entering further into the spiritual world.

This leads us to another aspect of the training in preparation for the elemental world. In the physical world, if we have an antipathy or an aversion to something then our natural inclination is to avoid that thing. However, in the elemental world, we have to learn to override our natural inclination of dealing with sympathy and antipathy in the usual way. Instead, we must learn to become a 'student' of what is shown to us. We must simply *be in a state of learning* through immersing ourselves in the pictures that reveal themselves. The soul immerses itself into each picture that is revealed, even when the soul is experiencing uncomfortable feelings.

There are several schooling exercises that can assist us in developing the capacity to override our common 'avoidance'-reactions to what is uncomfortable. One of these exercises is to recall an uncomfortable event, and learn to simply watch on.

This exercise helps to prepare us for the inevitable encounter with our own inner world. We need to think deeply of a situation that disturbed us, developing the situation again in our mind as fully as possible. Think of the details: where you were, what time of day it was, what you were wearing, what the environment was like, and what happened that disturbed you. All details need to be recreated vividly in the mind, preferably as a picture, but do not let *the soul's reaction* repeat the story of the event; rather, watch on as if you are observing someone else being disturbed. You may still feel uncomfortable inwardly, but don't let your soul run away from you. Keep looking on, watching the event, experiencing the event, without trying to change anything.

The leaders of the path of inner schooling have also suggested that attending certain plays, through which we can engage our soul-life in the twists and turns of the play, but at the same time remain in the audience simply watching on, strengthens our capacity for elemental encounters. Given the 'loosening' of the human soul-forces between the physical and elemental worlds that took place in the latter part of the 20th century, it is not surprising that today many people sit in front of screens, engaging in the drama and at the same time watching on. If we were able to use this technology as a training tool, we could strengthen ourselves and use it as inner schooling. Unfortunately, due to a weak inner life, most are just carried away by the errors and lies that play out in front of them, and indoctrinate their thinking in a direction leading further away from the strengthening that could be developed within themselves.

How difficult it must be for those who are not aware of the path, and who are not trained to manage the diversions from the progression of humanity that are upon us, and those diversions still to come—but who are nevertheless opening up to the elemental world as the collective shift brings us all across into this picture world.

Upon entering the elemental world, we encounter not only our own thoughts and feelings. If this were all we were to encounter, then it would not be necessary for there to be so many guards or levels of preparation required of us in order that we may become capable of integrating and managing the experiences which await us there. We also encounter the collective thought-atmosphere of humanity. This collective atmosphere is the result of human beings' inner relationships to the spiritual world.

There are several experiences that the student who has entered the elemental world may encounter, each of which will have a different effect depending on the preparation and capacities of the individual. One of those experiences is encountering fear. *Fear and anxiety* present themselves to the student of the inner work partly as a way of barring premature entry into the higher worlds. They also present themselves as a challenge to our ability to find a counterforce within ourselves. This experience of fear challenges us to cultivate *hope in humanity*. It is not our *personal* fear, but the *collective* fear that humanity has of the spiritual creativity of the living forces of the spirit that seek to work into our future becoming. We find the bravery to meet this fear in the knowledge of the path taught in the training.

If the student can 'see' in the elemental world, they may see this fear as a being. To begin with, this will instantly shock most people back into the waking day-consciousness of the personal self. It takes training to have the strength to simply watch on. The student may 'sense' it as a presence that causes deep fear within them; or may 'endure' it, in which case they will feel the fear arising as if it were their own.

We might experience this as a fear of what we need to recognize as spiritual truth, and of how far away our lives are from being in alignment with it. We also fear what may be asked of us as we behold the errors of our own ways. We fear what will become of us.

Those entering without training or the intensified strength of the ego will experience this fear blindly, in which case it will continue to produce inner anxiety and agitation. This is becoming a very common inner experience in our modern times. A recent study in Australia revealed that one in four Australian children feel worried or anxious most or all of the time. So many people are living with the results of loosening into the elemental world, but by and large they do not understand this process. Those who have knowledge of the path may also have a difficult time here, but for those who have no understanding, it is far more difficult; they are likely to turn to external measures in order to stop the experience. Many teenagers turning to substance use do so in order to stop the uncomfortable experiences of the inner life, only to find that they dig an even deeper trail into realms that may completely destabilize their minds. Because all drugs open one's consciousness without the normally-required inner strength, they in fact weaken the ego—in some cases even severing it. Drugs force the individual further into an inner condition which they have not won for themselves on the basis of inner work and readiness; therefore, the individual does not have the necessary strength to stand the ground in such conditions.

Through the knowledge and training of the path, we develop hope in the progress both of ourselves and of the world; we come to know that we must pass through certain challenges and that we need to *strengthen ourselves* if we are to reach calmer ground. Without knowledge, we turn towards medication or other methods of coping with our inner world, and then often attempt to return back to being 'normal' and being able to cope with life rather than attempting to progress further in order to transform the inner errors that produce our difficult experience of life.

We may also experience, rising up in us, a loathing or hatred towards the spiritual revelations when we come to recognize certain aspects of our way of being that need to undergo change or purification. We may refuse to acknowledge that we must change our ways; in this case, we hold on to the known and feel hatred towards the idea of transformation. Trying to keep hold of our personal preferences allows us to uphold the 'me'-self identity. Although the feeling-life may have the experience of being overwhelmed by the mountain that needs to be surmounted, the *enthusiasm* that we can feel for the path, and for the possibility of liberation, helps us onwards.

If we enter the elemental world unprepared, as is the case for so many young people in our time, then this unpreparedness leads to a rising up of loathing within us, and in consequence we feel inadequate in life. This continues into our inner world, and we feel inadequate about who we are and how we appear to others. It can become a self-hatred or a world-hatred that leads to destructive tendencies.

And the third of these forces that repel us from the threshold is *doubt* in the experiences, doubt in the power of the spirit over the external sense world. Here we need to engage ourselves with deeper commitment to a life of spiritual creativity. When we encounter this doubt unprepared, the dullness and worthlessness of our relationship to life well up within us. Nothing seems real or important; nothing seems worthwhile. We feel we are not able to have any impact on the world. We lose all faith in the purpose of existence. This can lead to deep depression or to a superficial striving that lacks individual purpose or interest. Thoughts may emerge, such as, *Why change myself if I cannot create change in the world?*, dampening our will for future possibilities.

We encounter these three beasts of our times—*fear, hatred,* and *doubt*—as a shadow-image of the collective thinking, feeling, and willing of humanity. If we 'see' them, they will arise as beasts of great difficulty, which we need to pass by, to overcome. If we 'sense' them, we will begin to recognize their impact on our inner world and thus the inner challenges that humanity as a whole is up against. If we find ourselves 'enduring' them, then we are likely to be experiencing fear, loathing, and doubt as inner realities that are hard to bear.

Even the inner life of other human beings is not the end of what we have to contend with; we are not the only beings who have access to the spiritual worlds. In the elemental world, we also encounter elemental beings; this is their terrain. These beings are the ones who produce the pictures we see; they do so out of their own bodies. These pictures are formed and reformed by consciousnesses that have power over the elemental beings—and those who thus have power over the elemental beings include human beings as well as all the hierarchies (both the progressive and diverting powers) above the human kingdom.

We could easily ask, *Is the elemental world real?* For the elemental beings are presenting pictures that are actually images of the thought and feeling life of another being. The elemental beings do not act out of themselves, but act according to another being's consciousness.

We could also ask the same of our physical world. It is the conglomeration of elements that are brought together under certain laws in order to produce certain forms and things in the external world around us. But if we were to break it down to particles and atoms, what we would see would not be what is actually there.

Elemental beings only take up the shape and form of the consciousness that directs them. We would not see them if they did not produce the picture of someone else's making. It is a kind of 'semblance world,' for we do not meet the maker of the picture—only the pictures themselves. Yet to anyone encountering them, they seem more real than the grey thinking of physical life.

Elemental beings will reflect pictures of our own thinking and feeling. When we have passed through the initial entry into this elemental world, the pictures we will see are pictures of humanity's thinking. If we pass through this level of the elemental world, we can receive pictures of the thinking and feeling of higher beings. The elemental beings produce the picture; the picture is not a reality, but an image stemming from the one who thus thinks into the picture-world. Therefore, it is easier to 'see' the elemental world than it is to 'read' it. Each picture is like a 'letter,' but not the being that is writing the 'word.' We only encounter the beings behind the pictures once we have entered the spiritual world.

To check *from whom* the pictures we 'see' or 'sense' are arising, we can change our own feeling life. If, in changing our inner feeling to loving feelings, the picture we are see-ing then changes into something pleasant *as a response,* this is a sign that what we are seeing stems from a source outside our own making. Something that is *outside* of our own consciousness, and expressing itself in the elemental world, must change in response to us. If the picture *does not change* into something pleasant as a response to our change in inner feeling activity, but continues to present disturbing images even when we are feeling loving qualities, then we can know that the picture has arisen from *our own* inner world.

The elemental beings who are presenting the pictures must present them according to the inner power of the force of soul that is influencing them. If we have *no power* over a soul force within us, then when we change the inner feeling we bring towards the picture, that picture will remain unchanged because we do not have governance over that soul force in ourselves. This unchanged picture continues to show us our inner reality in the elemental world. If an image arises that cannot be changed into something helpful, this is an indication of disturbances or untruths in our own inner life. This is very useful for us, as it allows us to see what still lives within ourselves. For in this elemental mirror-world, the mirror cannot lie.

If we do pass through the initial stages of the elemental world, we may also, through a certain training, encounter the group souls of the animal kingdom, as they also have a home in the elemental world. The animal-like pictures often break into our inner seeing. This is particularly the case for meat-eaters. This is not to promote vegetarianism, but it is just a fact that holds true if you carry the consciousness of animals within you; and that will be the case if you eat them. This is true of all that we 'eat'; those forces will not only show themselves within us, but they will also draw us to the realm in which they belong. This can also make sense of why young children of a meat-eating family do not need to be given animal flesh, or only in a very limited amount, until they reach a certain age.

Foods such as bone broths and bone marrow are the most directly connected to the animal's consciousness. It is true that the children fed on these diets will look etherically 'plumped up' by such foods, but their consciousness is being drawn into realms that are not actually helpful for the young child. What we eat affects our journey into higher realms. Eating animals makes a meditative life harder; it has a 'crowding' affect on our inner clarity through what then has to be met in the elemental world. Many teachers have spoken about the inner consequences of our unhealthy relationship to the animal kingdom, some more intensely than others.[25] An extensive research of Rudolf Steiner's work on our relationship to the animal kingdom can be found in the book *The Redemption of the Animals* by Douglas Sloan.[26] The following poem by Hafiz speaks of this in a lighter way as a part of what we will have to be responsible for or 'tidy up' in the elemental world:[27]

One of the dumbest things you can do is backbite an animal, or a human being.

Reason is: Besides the fact that an animal who is feeling grouchy that day might bite you back ...

whenever you speak ill of any living creature something of their shadow might fall on you.

Some unwanted impressions of theirs could spill on your floor,

and I imagine you are busy enough trying to keep things tidy.

Once, in the distant past, all the Indigenous and First Nation peoples had a clear and direct opening into the elemental world. At that time, their connection to this world was clarified and very different from how we experience it in the present age. They could make use of the shape-shifting, metamorphic nature of the elemental world in order to unite with the group souls of the animal kingdom, and thereby perceive what that animal consciousness perceived. Their inner work in the distant past was based on the elemental world. In contemplating the indigenous artifacts, masks, and headdresses, we can perceive the kinds of encounters that took place in this realm.

In those times, the consciousness of these people was not the waking day-consciousness of today; they once lived and breathed with the elemental realities just as we now live and breathe with physical realities. For these people, the elemental realities were far more real than physical life. Here, in the elemental world, they would also meet the thoughts of their ancestors. This was another direct experience of 'living with' the elemental plane of consciousness. For in the elemental world, the 'shell' of the last life of every person who dies is left behind. They could connect with the ancestors in order to help them direct their lives. In our time, what 'psychics' often communicate with is only the 'shell' of the individuality's last life, which is left behind before the soul passes through the threshold of the true spiritual world. The true being—the 'I', together with the soul-capacities—is the 'eternal' element that moves forward.

The 'shell' is left behind. There is a lot of fascination around working with these shells, but this is not the work of the true spiritual scientist.

For the student of the inner work, entering a 'shell' of another is the most peculiar of all the elemental experiences. For thereby we enter into the memory-life of another individual, and this momentarily becomes our memory life. We can begin to have thoughts that are not our own, and yet, they are based on memories with which we feel completely unified. Without this knowledge, we may think we have tapped into one of our past lives. However, this is someone else's past life, and generally, as with all elemental experiences, should not become a distraction or diversion, but an opportunity for us to strengthen ourselves against delusion.

The so-called magicians, wizards, and witches have always worked towards influencing the pictures that are perceptible in the elemental world. The staff or wand carried by the wizard is a picture-form of the elemental backbone that has been achieved through gaining not only access, but mastery, over parts of this world and the elemental beings who serve there. Elemental beings find it hard to play with or trick anyone who has established a foothold in this world through attaining the elemental backbone. But they can do so with anyone not having such a protection.

In the past, the magicians of the elemental world learned to work towards compelling those pictures to come to manifestation in the physical world, thereby commanding their service through their mastery over the thought world. If we were at a different stage in human development, invoking pictures from the elemental world might be regarded as an appropriate form of initiatory training; but we have moved on from that, and no true spiritual scientist would dabble in these realms.

In the past, the physical world was the battleground of the spirit between the powers of good and evil. Now, however, the initiate is more concerned with the task of transforming the nature of the negative thought-substance into the positive, in order to make the way clearer for those who will be affected by this thought substance upon their entry into the condition of elemental bombardment. The elemental world is the new battleground and many are entering unprepared, without their elemental backbone developed.

The students of initiation now battle in order that the good may continue to have a place in the elemental world. This means that as we enter into the realm of thought-life, alongside the thoughts of materialism and selfishness will be thoughts of the good, of the harmonious, and of the truth, which are consistently given from the spiritual worlds by the masters of wisdom and harmony and the beings of progression.

Of course, the initiates cannot do this for the individual's inner life, as each must be responsible as an individual. Each must clear up their own inner life for themselves, as that is what develops the capacity further and supports the way for others. However, the initiates and those in training do continue to change the nature of the erroneous thoughts, to work against the onslaught of erroneous activity with which the adversaries are filling the elemental world. The adversaries fill the elemental world with thoughts and pictures of diversion; the initiates, with thoughts and pictures of the true, the beautiful, and the good.

The true spiritual scientist is not interested in achieving any power in the elemental world. The spiritual scientist is seeking to participate in the true spiritual world, seeking to work with the spirits of progression who wish to guide humanity forward. Although much personal gain can be achieved through accessing power over the elemental world, this self-gain is a temptation that true seekers on the path of initiation train themselves to overcome.

Candidates for initiation may need to learn certain tools, such as the capacity to block negative thought-patterns and feelings that assail us in the elemental world; however, their true task is to change the nature of the thought-substance so that it may align with the good that is traced out in the true spiritual world.

Inner exercises—for example, working with the image of the *caduceus,* or the *rose cross*—have this protecting effect. The use of the *pentagram* is particularly powerful. But all of these must be utilized in the right way.

As mentioned above, the candidate for initiation recognizes that they are constantly up against erroneous thoughts that sweep through the collective consciousness and attack humanity in a blind, unseeing battle.

Many people live out of these errors, which are perpetuated by the mass-beliefs. Take the belief about passing exams; our school systems are in fact devising all sorts of ways *not* to healthily educate children, but to educate them with the aim of making them pass the examinations.

> When someone today—please take what I am now saying as a really serious matter—has learnt to think in a way perfectly adapted to meeting the demands of school examinations, whereby they acquire habits of thought that enable them to pass academic tests with flying colors—then their reasoning faculty will be so undermined that even if millions of experiences of the supersensible world were handed to them on a platter, they would be as little able to notice them as you would be able to physically see the objects in a dark room. For what makes human beings fit to cope with the demands of this materialistic age darkens the space in which the supersensible worlds come towards them.[28]

Through developing inner faculties, we begin to recognize the difference between truth and the mere opinions of other human beings, as well as the difference between truth and mere opinion in the context of the collective consciousness that surrounds us.

This leads us to another preparation for the elemental world. We must begin to fill our soul-content with truths arising from the eternal, and not from the transient world. This can be done in several ways: studying the esoteric pictures and lessons allows our soul to imbue itself with thoughts of the eternal and spiritual world. The verses and mantras also enable our soul to do this, as do the main exercises, such as the rose cross meditation. We are schooled in preparation for what we will experience as the soul undergoes transformation. If we only school our soul-life to work in the sense-world, then it will not be given the preparation required for the supersensible world.

All of these aspects present challenges to the student of the inner work, but the greatest challenge of all comes from the encounter with our own *'double.'*[29] In the elemental world, we not only encounter the erroneous thoughts of our current life, but our karmic imbalances are also revealed. When the student has developed far enough into the elemental world—and *before* crossing the threshold into the spiritual world—the necessary encounter with the double will arise. It is necessary, for in perceiving the double, our errors are thereby left at the threshold to the spiritual world.

There are three ways in which to pass through the elemental world in order to gain access into the spiritual world: first, by plunging into the thought-pictures and coming through to the other side; second, by diving into the feeling-pictures and emerging into the spiritual world; or, third, by using the might of your will to extinguish the elemental pictures, and through this might, taking yourself across the threshold.

This capacity to 'extinguish' must be prepared through the meditative practice. It is this capacity that is required to pass the encounter with the double.

In meditative training, we are also taught to eliminate the pictures that we have built up. This becomes a necessity in the elemental world, for we need to be able to extinguish the pictures before us. Life in the elemental world is not like that of the physical world, where when we have had our fill of physical life we simply go to sleep—and through sleep, unconsciously enter into other realms of being. Once we are in the elemental world, in order to consciously pass into further realms, we have to put our inner picture-life 'to sleep' or extinguish it entirely. Through this, we may pass through the elemental world into the lower spiritual world.

We are training ourselves to develop two principal capacities: the capacities to *enter* and *pass through* the elemental world. Without the necessary capacities, we would naturally avoid entering unknown territory if we could. Without the necessary preparations—even if through the common loosening of the veils we stumble into this world, as so many are prone to do—we would not be able to pass onwards to the true spiritual world.

Entering the elemental world and not having the proper training can cause great difficulties in the soul. Encountering any of these forces unconsciously can create deep anxiety or soul-disturbances. An unconscious encounter with the double induces depression. The thoughts intensify and the feelings grow out of control. Without having undergone preparation, it is hard to manage one's own soul in the elemental world, and harder still to pass through it. As has been described, this unmanageability of the inner life is becoming increasingly prevalent in the world. Whether we want to or not, whether we are prepared or not, we are crossing this threshold.

Even before any 'seeing' within the elemental worlds begins, the thinking belonging to the physical world now appears dead in comparison to the intensified, living elemental world. In the elemental world, the soul activities are now vibrant, externalized experiences that we can see, sense, and participate in. In this supersensible world, the ego does not have the physical body to provide it with a sense of 'I'-consciousness, and therefore it needs to have been strengthened in order to be able to remain a steady point amidst the constant movement of elemental life.

In the physical world, the bodily sheaths contain the ego as a personality. In the elemental world, the personality needs to be transformed. In the state of lucid dreaming, the personality continues to call the shots, to react and respond. The so-called 'astral travel' techniques are also to be avoided, because they involve trying to keep the personality intact whilst opening into altered states. This will only lead to detrimental errors of experience.

Three main capacities must be developed in order to experience other worlds of consciousness. The *first* is that we *gain strength over our own soul forces*: that we gain the ability to control and order our inner thinking, feeling, and willing. This develops the individual ego-capacity. The ego-capacity required for the elemental world is far greater than that required in daily life.

The *second* capacity we need may be described as the *wings of reverence*, which enable us to pass into the world of spirit: to know we are not the 'be all and end all' of consciousness but that higher, benevolent beings support us on our path onwards.

The *third* capacity is to be able to *develop the organs of perception* that are to be sculpted from the freed soul forces. These organs are not developed in the physical world, nor in the elemental world, but in the lower spiritual world.

3

INNER DEVELOPMENT FOR THE SPIRITUAL WORLD

"The eye was made by the light, for the light, so that the inner light may emerge to meet the outer light." [30]

— *J. W. v. GOETHE*

The organs of spiritual perception are created by the spirit, for the spirit, so that the inner spirit may emerge to meet the outer spirit.

On the path of initiation, as we work towards the fullness of our spiritual reality we learn to be awake to other realms of consciousness. When the ego or 'I'-being can no longer rely on the bodily sheaths to provide it with the point of self-awareness, it must then develop this capacity out of itself; it must develop its 'I'-consciousness to a greater degree. The soul-life, which enables us to experience the world around ourselves, is attuned to and developed for its experiences in the physical world through its connection with the bodily sheaths. In order that it may become an organ of perception for other worlds, the soul-life must undergo further transformation. In the esoteric schooling, the transformation of the soul is called "the development of the devachanic organs." These are the 'lotus flowers' or 'chakras.' The healthy, ordered development of the petals of the lotus flowers, of the spokes of the chakras, takes place in the spiritual world itself. The organs of perception are created in the same world that they are equipped to perceive. A gestation period is necessary for their harmonious forming, so that thereby we may experience a full spiritual life. The more the individual is able to rest in tranquility and peace during the time of spiritual gestation, the more readily can the soul-organs for spiritual perception be created by the spiritual world.

The soul-organs are fashioned out of soul substance. We are responsible for offering this substance which is to be worked upon. The only substance that can be fashioned into the harmonious organs of perception is the substance that belongs to and resounds with the spiritual world. It is through the transformation of the soul that instead of the soul relating on the basis of sympathies and antipathies, it becomes an organ of deeper experience.

When a human being uses pleasure and displeasure in such a way that they become organs of transmission [i.e., opportunities to learn about the nature of things],[31] these qualities build up for that person, within their soul, the actual organs through which the soul-world opens up to view. The eye can serve the body only by being an organ for the transmission of sense impressions. Pleasure and pain become the *eyes of the soul* when they cease to be of value merely to themselves and begin to reveal to one's soul the other soul outside it.[32]

When we first enter into the *lower spiritual world*, we leave behind the mirror-picturing of the elemental world, and enter the world in which the inner soul life no longer sees itself reflected in pictures of living expression—as was the case in the elemental world—but exists now as *pure soul-activity*.

This world is unlike the sense world, and bears no resemblance to sense experience. Even the elemental world has familiar images that could be related to the sense world around us; but in the lower spiritual world, we are at first entirely alone in the emptiness. The sense-impressions, and the inner pictures that result from those impressions, are all left behind us; all that remains as life is the soul's deeper living *activity*.

From the present time onward, it will be impossible for the human being to acquire any real self-knowledge, or feeling for their own being, without approaching the science of initiation; for the forces out of which human nature actually takes shape are nowhere contained in what the human being is able to know or experience in the material world.[33]

The ego-sheath is also relinquished, and the 'higher I,' its spiritual counterpart, continues on the journey of initiation. It is always present in the lower spiritual world, but only to the degree corresponding to our level of development. Through the right crossing, the personal and material content of the soul is left behind at the gates of the spiritual world; only its deeper activity passes on. The 'higher I,' along with the purer activities of soul, are residents of this realm; they feel 'at home' in the lower spiritual world. During the meditative practice, the student has been working towards this by means of the *first 'extinguishing,'* which enables us to leave behind all the *content* of the exercise, and after which only *soul activity* remains. (See *The Inner Work Path*.[34])

It is only in the upper or 'higher' spiritual world that the 'I' alone exists; in this realm, we leave behind even the soul's activity. This has been prepared for through the *second 'extinguishing'* in the meditative practice.

We do not wish to pass by the elemental world without first using it to purify all that cannot enter into the pure soul world; and likewise, we do not wish to pass through the lower spiritual world without first becoming a citizen of that spiritual life. It is here, in the lower spiritual world that the student is for the first time aware of other beings, of other consciousnesses. The student may for the first time have the recognition, *"I am a spiritual being among spiritual beings."*

On the true schooling path, we enter into the world of beings, the hierarchies who are actively supporting the progression of humanity. This School is under the guidance of the current leading Arche, Michael, and is therefore termed the *Michael School*. The Archai work for the progression of all of humanity, whereas the Archangels work for the progression of groups or streams within humanity and the Angels for the progression of the individuals within those streams. They are a community of spiritual beings that directly supports humanity's evolution.

All beings participating in the progression and evolution of humanity work within the Michael School, although many students of this true School may not know it by this name.

These beings can reveal themselves only if the students carry within them, in soul activity, the language and laws corresponding to these beings. There are some students who rise into the spirit and then say, "nothing exists"; and this is real for them. We remain as hermits in the world of spirit for as long as we have not embodied the language in which the beings of this world can communicate with us, revealing their presence.

If we were to enter the spirit realm with only that which we have discovered in the physical and elemental worlds, then we would be confronting nothingness.[35]

In order to recognize the stages that are developed in this lower spiritual world, we must first understand what we can take with us into it. This is the world of a deeper soul activity, by means of which spiritual beings reveal themselves through spiritual 'conversation.'

This speech is not human speech. It is neither English, nor German, nor any language other than the 'language' of the deeper soul life.

The aphorism from *Light on the Path* that can guide us correctly here states:

Before the voice can speak in the presence of the Masters it must have lost the power to wound.[36]

The primary element of any 'wounding' is the influence of the 'me'-self that wants to adulterate the spirit. Through this path, the 'me'-self has been purified. The life of inner training and the elemental world have helped us with this. We have left behind at the threshold all that should not come with us, because we have been able to see it. In seeing it, it is not yet transformed in us, but it loses all power over us.

As difficult as the elemental world is, it safeguards us from a self-deceptive, premature crossing; in this way, the Guardian of the Threshold works to guide us into the true schooling that works on behalf of all humanity.

However there is also a 'wounding' that still needs to be corrected within the spiritual world itself, and that can indeed be corrected here: this second 'wounding' is the degree of disharmony and lack of wisdom that the soul still contains. This is adjusted through our regular entry into the place where the 'masters of wisdom and harmony' reside.

The 'language' that the soul can 'hear' can be understood in seven expressions. However, these must be understood as activities of the soul, and as having nothing to do with sense-perceptible realities. We may come closer to the understanding of this 'language' in the following words from the Mystery Dramas: "At this place words are deeds, and further deeds must follow them."[37]

We are able to develop the substance for this language through an inner training that is hidden from the abstract intellect: by means of the verses, mantras, and exercises.

Behind the 'clothing' of the *content* of the exercise, verse, or mantra, there exist seven 'portals,' which school our deeper soul work, as doorways or entry-points into the language of the lower spiritual world. For the soul that is ready to learn 'soul language,' the verses also train us to develop capacities in a different way than they did in relation to our development in the elemental world or sense world.

We are now without the picture-creating substance of the elemental world. What is left when there is neither physical substance nor elemental substance? Here there exists nothing other than the *capacity* of the soul and the 'I'-consciousness.

We can begin to explore what is required of all who wish to participate and to be active within this richer inner world. Even though each individual will find the 'portal of entry' that speaks most clearly to them individually, it is still useful to explore all of the portals, as this also helps us to understand the way in which higher beings communicate or reveal themselves.

Humanity must develop an awareness of not being of this earth, and this must grow stronger and stronger. In the future, human beings must walk on this earth who say to themselves: 'Yes, at birth I enter into a physical body, but this is a transitional stage. I really remain in the spiritual world. I am conscious that only a part of my essential nature is united with the earth, and that, with the whole of this my essential nature, I never leave the world in which I dwelt between death and rebirth.'

A feeling of belonging to the spiritual world must develop in us.[38]

To begin with, the seven portals can simply be named: *color, measure, number, sound, direction, movement,* and *form*. Although we never experience these portals in isolation, we can begin to explore them in order to understand the soul-activity that is being developed and schooled by each one. Working with them serves to develop the only activity that can be taken with the student into the spiritual world.

Even if it has been translated into various languages, a true esoteric verse or mantra will not risk having all of its portals closed. Entry via one portal will allow the spirit to also school us in the others. If the candidate of initiation has achieved the process of soul-development, then all true spiritual works become alive for that student in a way that cannot be obscured or hindered through translation.

You must take the meditative life with such strength into your soul that through this meditative life you grasp the world differently.[39]

This is an extensive study that requires commitment and effort; many of these studies will need to be taken up separately from the meditative practice if we wish to work with them dynamically *within* the meditative practice. To begin exploring these portals as 'soul language,' we can return to our verse. This verse was first given in Sanskrit:

More radiant than the sun,
Purer than the snow,
Finer than the ether
Is the self,
Spirit in my heart.
I am this self,
This self am I.[40]

THE PORTAL OF COLOR OR MOOD

Each verse or mantra has a *mood*, and it is the mood
that is continued *within the soul* after the verse is extin-
guished. In this verse, we could experience the *'mood
activity'* of the individual lines—such as the 'yellow' that
the verse points us to with the words *"More radiant
than the sun"*—as a part of the working *soul language*
of this verse; at the same time, if we follow the mood
of the verse we can see other soul-colors speaking. We
can experience that there is a change of mood between
the first and second halves of the verse. The 'color' or
mood contributes to the developing soul-language; this
is the quality of communication that exists in the lower
spiritual world. There, it is only soul-activity that we can
take with us; and this activity is then worked upon in
that region.

To begin with, *color* is an easier portal, as most people
recognize the different activities that color induces in the
soul. For many people, this is only a fine 'whisper' of
experience until the soul has been trained in the qualities
of activity that result from the experiences of different

colors. Part of the inner training may involve carrying out exercises that serve to develop this ability.

Exercise in color activity

When we look at a source of light through the veil of a red film, it produces a different activity in our inner world than if we practice the same exercise through a blue or a yellow film.

We can try this with anything that lets in the light—such as colored glass bottles, color projected through light onto a surface—or through painting.

The soul activity is easier to perceive if we compare the differing qualities of inner experience resulting from these three colors. Working in turn with each color, try to find a word that can express the inner activity produced by the color.

The word we give is not the activity, but points to the activity.

We may experience something like 'strength' or 'vitality' with the activity of red, whereas blue produces 'peace' and 'quietness.' Yellow's activity might be described as 'clarity' or 'striving.' The word is not the activity; it is only the 'clothing' we place upon the activity in order to convey it to another. Even though I have suggested some words here as examples, it is not about finding the right word but attuning to the soul-activity that engages differently in each case, thus creating an inner mood activated by the given color.

When we work with the activity contained in the line, *"More radiant than the sun,"* we will experience a different quality of inner 'streaming' than with *"Purer than the snow"* or *"Finer than the ether."* Ultimately, when we drop the outer words of the verse, the *activity* should still be present within us: the overall mood of the verse will resound within us even when the words are gone.

The Portal of Measure, Meter, or Rhythm

Measure or *rhythm* is also hidden in most verses. In some verses, we find the *iambic* rhythm. The iambic meter takes us from the valleys to the heights of the gods; the soul ascends with this rhythm of *short-long, short-long, short-long.* The *trochaic* meter takes the soul from the heights to the valley with its *long-short, long-short, long-short* meter; whereas the *spondaic* meter holds the soul half-way between the valley and the heights with its rhythm of *long-long, long-long, long-long.* These three are the most common rhythms, and they already exist in the human heart.

One of the most extraordinary things about the majesty of the verses is that *the rhythm will reflect the 'direction' of the meaning of the words.* When we come back to the verse, we can experience that the rhythm changes at points where the verse is speaking to our deeper soul-world. Now, following the rhythm, we can hear that the first three lines work together:

More radiant than the sun,
Purer than the snow,
Finer than the ether

Then, we have a change in the next measure:

Is the self,

Then, back to three more 'related' measures:

Spirit in my heart.
I am this self,
This self am I.[41]

When we engage artistically with the verse's meaning, we allow the deep soul-nourishment to enter our being; we are inwardly moved. Do we inwardly experience the change as the verse changes? It is not about working out which 'meter' is at work, but rather engaging with the deeper schooling of the verse.

THE PORTAL OF NUMBER

In order to see how the 'number law' works, we must look individually at the numbers and their esoteric meaning. Some of the older esoteric schools stressed the necessity of immersing oneself in 'number laws.' The Pythagorean School was one that stressed this portal, as did Rudolf Steiner in describing the secrets of the threshold:

A soul that wants to prepare itself for knowledge of the spiritual world gradually begins to search everywhere in the world, at every point that can be reached, for the understanding of number [...].[42]

Here the numbers are represented also in the form of signs or symbols, in order to allow us to be affected by number without thinking that it merely represents earthly, abstract numbers. Each number has a different effect on our soul's activity. We should not immerse ourselves in these numbers until we have a sense of all seven and can move between them.

Number 1: the starting point •

It is very difficult for the human soul to comprehend the number *one* because in the world of the senses, there is no inner experience of *one* or *oneness*. Even the number *two* is not really comprehended by the human soul, although all that we do see and experience in the material world appears to us in the form of *duality*. Duality reveals itself *in relationship*; therefore, the human soul begins to understand only when reaching the number *three*. Esoterically, the number *one* represents *God, the all*, and *the everything*. This number designates the indivisible unity of the spirit. Nothing else exists but *one*.

Number 2: the line |

Esoterically, the number *two* is the first that comes into the state of *separation*. There is no longer a unity; *two* manifests the *duality*. *Two* is the number of *revelation*. Whatever reveals itself must do so via the number *two*—this is even true of the unseen forces of electricity and magnetism. If it is *known*, it is therefore revealed *in duality*. Development itself moves between involution and evolution; behind this, the creative godhead, which cannot be revealed as *one*, can express itself as *three*.

Number 3: the divine creates (the triangle)

With the number *two*, there is a 'middle space,' there is a relationship between the two things; therefore, the *two* becomes *three*, as the third is the relationship between the two things. The divine participates through the number *three*. Esoterically, the number *three* is where the divine can reveal itself, between the duality of the *two*; for where there are *two*, a third may enter. The number *three* is deeply significant for the student of the inner work; it is said to be the most significant number to be contemplated and understood. The polarities stand in opposition. The divine reveals itself in the number *three*; this is why God can be known more clearly in the world as a *trinity*.

In order to be known, the *one* (the unknowable God-number) can enter between the *two* (the revelation number). In this, we can see how the divine is revealed through the polarities. Without the division, the unknowable would not be able to be known.

Number 4: the cross

The number *four* is where life becomes manifest; it is factual and perceptible.

The earth is the fourth embodiment of creation. It is creation in its outer manifestation. All that manifests in the physical world is manifest through *four*.

When Rudolf Steiner spoke about who would be the true carriers of anthroposophy—in a sense, his successors—he said it would be the 4 × 12 people in whom the *Michael Thought* becomes fully alive.[43] When an initiate speaks in this way, he does not mean 48 people: 4 × 12 indicates that it will be those people with whom the divine is able to participate through the realm of the Michael School—and from there, working into the physically manifested world. Ultimately, with these words Rudolf Steiner expresses what he himself has done, and indicates the realm out of which leaders of the future must work in this Michaelic age. For others to recognise these individuals, they must have awoken this capacity to some degree within themselves.

Number 5: the pentagram

The number *five* is often seen as the number of crisis, dramatic change, or of a definite turning point.

The pentagram has been used esoterically as a form of protection from the potential turmoil of the number five, bringing order to it. This is the sign borne by the purified soul that moves through the elemental world, into which it may likewise convey the influence of order. It indicates that all the elements are harmonized, and they can only become thus harmonized through the spiritual activity of the soul working down into the etheric body and passing on or impressing this harmony into it. The fifth element, *spirit,* is added to the four others of *earth, water, air,* and *fire.* It is the star found on the Christmas tree, won by the initiates of the degree that walks the path of the sun.

The esoteric arts carry many of these spiritual laws within them. They work by speaking directly to the soul and bypassing our abstract intellect. Think of the Sistine Madonna by Raphael. This is a deeply esoteric picture. Through contemplation, it works upon the soul; and at the same time, it depicts in picture-form what it wants to express in the soul—thereby working, as true esoteric works do, on several levels at once. We can see the Madonna carrying the child through the veils that separate the two worlds; she is not touching the physical, and the cherubs at the bottom show that she is not in the earthly world. She stands there, emerging through the elemental world from out of the spirit. In her arms, the Christ child gazes strongly towards the future. We may also see that there is a pentagram, and may even see the direction it is headed.

In being assessed within the Rosicrucian School, candidates would be given art like this in order to see what level of development speaks most clearly in them. In this way, the individual's previous development and schooling could be ascertained.

In our earthly world, there are Mysteries of the spirit that we can only access if we ourselves have the inner organs needed to become aware of them. One human being can cross the ocean and remain unchanged inwardly, whereas another takes the same journey and is transformed. One person can observe a sunset and say, "It's a pity there is not more purple on the left side; it would be better if there were," whilst another will be deeply, inwardly moved by the same experience. All depends on the inner capacity of the individual's soul.

Number 6: the six-pointed star

The six-pointed star is the sign for the conscious and full development in the lower spiritual world. It is the sign of the active relationship with the beings in the lower spiritual world. Not only can we hear and receive—and grow in that activity of receiving—but in the *six* we can *give*; here, the initiate has voice to bring forward out of themselves that which will be progressive for humanity. It is the number of harmony between the above and below. Human life begins to live in accord with the truths that are traced out in the spiritual world not only inwardly, but also outwardly: *As above, so below.*

Number 7: the six-pointed star with a point in the center

The final perfection of the human being is present in the number *seven*; it is not to be seen as completion, but rather *perfection*. The candidate of initiation seeks this perfection in the process of working diligently through all stages of transformation. The *point*, which we first saw as the symbol of number *one*, is now back, in the center of the six-pointed star. The jewel is in the lotus. When T. Subba Row[44] was asked how long it would take until a person awakens, he gave the answer: "seven months, seven years, or seven lifetimes." His answer was the answer of the deep esotericist: When perfection has been reached.

When we immerse ourselves in number and number law, this influence speaks to the soul even though we may know nothing of it consciously. Firstly, there are seven lines to the verse below; many of the esoteric verses have seven lines. Most of the mantras are 3 × 7 lines. This is number law at work; it is a soul language that we gradually allow to affect us. Try immersing yourself in the number *three*; it has a different living inner activity for us than the number *four* or any of the other numbers. Each number has an activity that the deeper aspect of the soul recognizes.

When we look at the verse again from the perspective of number law, not only do we experience the 'law of seven,'

which takes us through one full cycle, but we also experience the difference between the first three lines and the
next four lines. If we let the verse speak to us, we begin
to see that we could experience this verse as a '313' verse
that has also been expressed in the meter of the verse.

More radiant than the sun,
Purer than the snow,
Finer than the ether

Is the self,

Spirit in my heart.
I am this self,
This self am I.[45]

The effect that the number has on the soul does not
stand alone; there is also the effect of the meter, which
instructs us that this is a *three-one-three* verse.

No one who engages with this verse from the perspective of number law, and with the corresponding level of
inner activity, could ever question which 'self' is being referred to. For the line *"Is the self"* stands as a *one*-num-
ber-activity within the context of the verse, and the soul
knows that number *one* is the 'God number.' It cannot
mean the everyday self. It is the greater self—not the personal self—that is being spoken of.

Here we see how the words, the meter, and the number
all speak of and point to the same truth. Whether we know
it or not, this truth is registered deep within the soul; and
over time, it has the effect of working upon the soul, thus

schooling it further. But this truth can work further only if we give ourselves deeply to the verse. If we dissect it with the intellect, it remains a closed door.

THE PORTAL OF SOUND

"When all the strings of my life will be tuned, my Master, then at every touch of thine will come the music of love." —Rabindranath Tagore [46]

Sound can sometimes be 'lost in translation.' The combining of vowels and the forming of consonants have an extraordinary effect on the soul-life, the full significance of which we do not yet recognize. The sounding and the resounding effect of the sounds in a verse are a part of the soul-conversation. This may require much deeper study, because it is the central portal. We hear the harmony of the spheres through this evolving.

Some sound-meditations need to be worked with in their original language, such as this mantra in Sanskrit:

Om mani padme Hum.

It is sounded in seven syllables, as:

A-um ma ni pad me Hum

The translations cannot recreate this 'sound portal'— for example, an English translation is: *"the jewel in the lotus."* This sound mantra would be worked with in untranslated form, because it is *primarily* a sound mantra—even though it also carries the iambic meter and the number *seven*, and creates a certain color or mood.

Certain other esoteric sayings also carry more power in their original language, such as:

Ex Deo nascimur,
In Christo morimor,
Per Spiritum Sanctum reviviscimus.

There are also other sound exercises given with the purpose of awakening our 'sound capacity,' such as the following:

The students have also to bestow a further care on the world of sound. One must discriminate between sounds that are produced by the so-called inert (lifeless) bodies—for instance, a bell, or a musical instrument, or a falling mass—and those which proceed from a living creature (an animal or a human being). When a bell is struck, we hear the sound and connect a pleasant feeling with it; but when we hear the cry of an animal, we can, besides our own feeling, detect through it the manifestation of an inward experience of the animal, whether of pleasure or pain. It is with the latter kind of sound that the students set to work. They must concentrate their whole attention on the fact that the sound tells them of something that lies outside their own soul. They must immerse themselves in this foreign thing. They must closely unite their own feeling with the pleasure or pain of which the sound tells them. They must get beyond the point of caring whether, for them, the sound is pleasant or unpleasant, agreeable or disagreeable, and their soul must be filled with whatever is occurring in the being from which the sound proceeds. Through such exercises, if systematically and deliberately performed, the students will develop within themselves the faculty of intermingling, as it were, with the being from which the sound proceeds.[47]

Sound is something that is communicated, and it can be the speech of the hierarchies—however, not as audible wavelengths of sound, but as inner activity. In this next sound meditation, we are given the power of the sound of *Yahweh*.

SOUND MEDITATION

In this meditation, you sound the vowels aloud, and then inwardly imagine and experience the inner indications:[48]

I   (Stillness within you)

A (You open to the world, which speaks)

O (The Angels come and join hands)

U (The Second Hierarchy follows, surrounding you with light)

E   (The First Hierarchy comes, burning you with fire)

The Portal of Direction

Direction is sometimes obvious, but often it is more disguised than the other portals—although it is not less important.

Just like all the portals, inwardly the deeper soul already has some relationship to *direction*. Close your eyes and draw a cross in front of yourself. Which way did you draw it?

From somewhere within us, we already know to start at the top of the cross and draw down to the bottom, even though it is in mid-air. Now try drawing the line from the bottom up to the top, and feel how different that direction is. Once we learn *direction*, we begin to open up an inner quality that we may never before have accessed.

The pentagram, for instance, activates different elements according to the direction used. The *earthly stream* is activated and expressed when we draw it starting at the head of the pentagram and moving to the right foot, the left hand, then the right hand, then the left foot, and back to the head. The *fiery stream* is activated when we work with the pentagram in the opposite direction, starting at the head, to the left foot, and so forth. The *airy stream* starts at the left hand and moves to the right hand first, then the left foot, then the head, then the right foot, and back to the left hand. The *watery stream* moves in the opposite direction, the starting point being at the right hand.

A pentagram exercise: for meeting the world[49]

This exercise should be done in the morning; it can be very energizing. It is a fifteen-minute exercise—not by the clock, but by your inner timing.

5 minutes: Contemplate these words: *Everything that happens around me, and everything that happens to me, is necessary.*

5 minutes: Concentrate on the eyes: *I will regard everything around me in this way.*
Concentrate on the heart, then extending towards the arms and then into the hands, with the words: *I will do in this way everything that should be done by me.*

5 minutes: Draw inwardly a bright yellow pentagram, starting from the forehead to the left foot, the right hand, the left hand, the right foot, and then back to the forehead.

Hold this bright yellow pentagram visually, inwardly, then concentrate on the words: *Strength in me.*

This exercise combines color, measure, number, sound, direction, movement, and form. Some of these elements are more strongly in evidence and others more weakly, but all are present. So much is expressed in this one exercise that it, like most others, is thereby able to work on the student according to the particular step they are on.

THE PORTAL OF MOVEMENT

Movement exists in every place where the soul is in a state of activity. Activity requires movement; if there is no movement, there is no activity.

Just as *number* and *measure* exist side by side, the same is true of *direction* and *movement*. We can try to study movement in isolation from the other qualities—for example, the movement of how a piece of music moves within the soul—but with every instance of movement, other portals are likewise at work. The best way to understand the quality of *'esoteric movement'* is through eurythmy. Eurythmy is recognized as the highest of the arts because it carries within it a strong relationship to all seven portals. With eurythmy we see how movement and sound are intimately linked. It reveals the mystery of the deep relationship between spiritual speech and soul activity in a form of expression that can be seen in the outer world. The arts are able to cultivate this insight in a living way; through eurythmy, we have the most intimate and profound of all the artistic expressions capable of showing to us, and thus preparing us for, the nature of experience in the lower spiritual world. When watching artistic eurythmy, we can imagine ourselves in the midst of the stage and in the midst of the beings moving around us, speaking, but without sound: *speaking with their very being.* This gives us a glimpse of the life of spiritual speech in the lower spiritual world; however, in this realm each movement creates something that continues to have life through the fact of its resounding into substance—substance which awaits a creative act in order that it may become something.

THE PORTAL OF FORM

Form is not only to be understood in terms of clear forms, such as that of the pentagram; rather, each verse has its own form. Some will leave clear, archetypal signs in the soul, whereas others leave a unique and uncommon form. Forms have a far stronger effect on us through the fact of our living with them every day. In experiencing architecture, we meet forms; and here we can let the forms work on us in a more obvious, outer sense.

How do the shapes of a window affect us? What line moves us towards the heavens? In the esoteric training, we may work with exercises such as this.

Begin by visualizing a five-pointed star; then, in your inner picture-thinking, change it into a six-pointed star. Do not simply start visualizing a six-pointed star, but transform the five pointed star *in form* so that it becomes the six-pointed star.

Forms or *signs* can also be brought into the body, for the body itself is a form.

One 'sign' belonging to the first grade of initiation is actually used by many unknowingly: that is *the bodily position of prayer*. By bringing reverence into the body through this sign, we affect our inner life. The bowing of the head, then the bringing of the hands together, and the bending of the knees, all in reverence, have a purifying effect.

Two signs belonging to the second grade involve forming a triangle with the hands: first below the navel, and then again above the head. The first triangle, pointed downwards, is in the region of the lower abdomen; one of the meanings of this triangle is to signify a commitment to practice. One meaning of the triangle made above the head, pointed upwards, is to signify uniting with the wisdom of the spirit. Here we have a combination of *form* with *direction, number,* and *movement.*

In the physical world, these spiritual truths may speak to us through the great arts. In the arts, we see a combination of several of these portals expressed together. The arts are what deeply nourish the human soul in the physical world; through them, everyone can be nourished by the substance of the communicated wisdom and harmony of the spiritual world.

These forces in our souls, which we become aware of in the course of the inner work, and with which we engage directly in the lower spiritual world, are divine forces. Through building and growing these forces, the higher spiritual world can be placed in us like a 'jewel in the lotus.'

We must seek within ourselves for those forces which are of a divine nature; for these forces have been implanted in us in the course of the world's becoming in order that we may use them, in order that we may receive God into our individual souls. We should not allow ourselves to resort to preaching about some external God, so that our souls can live in indolent repose on philistine sofas, of which we are so fond whenever it is a matter of the spiritual life.[50]

The inner training will serve to awaken each individual in their own way; for it is the *individual* in relationship to the work that is most essential. Each for themselves must walk the path. How can we bring ourselves into a deep, individual relationship to the inner work, and yet not resort to 'playing' with the wisdom concealed within it? Is it not in and through the *wisdom* that the deeper training takes place?

The majesty of the esoteric verses bypasses our egotism, bypasses our intellect, and works on schooling the soul so that it may resound with a soul-activity that is of the same substance and quality as the spiritual world. Often, people want to change the exercises according to their personal preferences—for example, not wanting to imagine seven roses in a ring around the rose-cross because it does not appeal to them or is felt to be too difficult. There are deep and meaningful reasons for why the seven roses are placed in a ring around the arms of the cross; placing them in any other way will produce different results.

Some people in Australia often think the exercises are too 'European,' and therefore want to replace the roses with Australian-native bush flowers. The rose-symbol has a certain effect that is essential for human beings of our time; by changing the flower, we change what the soul receives. By changing the symbols used due to our personal preferences, we are altering the exercise in a way that will not only produce different results, but may hinder progress.

Sometimes people refuse to read fairytales from Europe (some of which are, incidentally, full of these seven portals), saying that such fairy tales do not work in the southern hemisphere, or in the souls of children not born in Europe. This may be reasonable to say for the elemental world, but not the spiritual world. By saying such things, it shows how little we understand how the uniting activity of the spiritual world speaks and works. It shows how little we understand the eternal. Of course, it is also productive for school teachers to create their own stories; but we are unable to make up esoteric wisdom, as such wisdom is *given*. Sometimes the wisdom is given in children's fairy tales, feeding the child in a way that supersedes the qualities of land and country. There needs to be *seven* swans or *three* princes, the third being the youngest that wins the day. There are of course empty fairytales in the world, but some are full of wisdom that feeds the deeper soul's need.

Due to the necessity of spiritual development in our times, more and more people are taking up inner work. They recognize this necessity and are searching for exercises and training that will meet this growing need. At the same time, many are speaking on the topic of inner development, and courses that would not have used such a title in the past are now being called 'inner development' courses. Many wish to pass on their enthusiasm for meditation, some suggesting that students meditate on whatever 'pops into' their mind. Others recommend combining

exercises from various schools and indigenous tribal traditions, in a mix-and-match sort of fashion. Some doctors
are even prescribing inner exercises instead of medica-
ments in order to meet the needs of their patients. Do we
really know what effects the given practice is serving to
produce? What is our responsibility when giving out these
pictures and practices to others?

Do we know what we are doing when we bring in
personal soul-exercises that are not actually for spiritual
training, but designate them as such? It is becoming
particularly common that soul-exercises which serve to
strengthen the *personal* self within the physical world
are being promoted as meditations or 'esoteric inner
schooling.' With this trend, self-serving tendencies are
infiltrating genuine schooling.

People are becoming interested in, even fascinated
with, the elemental world, but without the necessary
development that creates the 'elemental backbone' needed
to work healthily within that world. Self-development
always requires strict training and the overcoming of all
desire to titillate ourselves. Now, with the opening of the
elemental world, we will see more diversions calling to the
human soul than ever before, because this is easier than
the hard work required for genuine development. Rudolf
Steiner warned that people will face the temptation of
becoming interested in having *any* experience over
waiting patiently and working towards genuine ones.

We all 'make things up' when we change the deep, esoteric work to suit our preferences and ourselves. We make
things up because we are all spiritually young; we have so

far to go in our relationship to spiritual unfolding, but we imagine we are already there because we can intellectually understand esoteric works. This alone cannot produce any spiritual results.

ON BEHALF OF LOVE
by Thomas Aquinas[51]

Every truth without exception—no matter
who makes it—is from God.

If a bird got accused of singing too early
in the morning,

if a lute began to magically play on its own
in the square
and the enchanting sounds it made drove a pair of young
      lovers
into a wild, public display of
passion,

if this lute and bird then got called before the inquisition
and their lives were literally at stake,

could not God walk up and say before the court,

"All acts of beauty are mine, all happen on the behalf
      of love"?

And while God was there, testifying for our heart's desires,
hopefully the judge would be astute enough
to brave a question,
that could go,

"Dear God, you say all acts of beauty are yours,
surely we can believe that. But what of all actions
we see in this world,
for is there any force in existence greater than the power
of your omnipresent hand?"

And God might have responded, "I like that question,"
adding, "May I ask you one as well?"

And then God would say,

"Have you ever been in a conversation when children
        entered
the room, and you then ceased speaking because your
wisdom knew they were not old enough to benefit—to
        understand?

As exquisite is your world, most everyone in it
is spiritually young.

Spirituality is love, and love never wars with the minute,
        the day,
one's self and others. Love would rather die
than maim a limb,
a wing.

Dear, anything that divides man from man,
earth from sky, light and dark, one religion from
        another...
O, I best keep silent, I see a child
just entered the
room."

How can we live intimately with our *individual* path, and yet commit our inner training to a path that has been handed down through the Esoteric School? Admittedly, it is difficult to achieve this in the age of the consciousness soul, but how could we legitimately think that we could progress by 'making up' the content of our training? How could the personality 'make up' that which will be used to school our eternal soul? All the great teachers, including Rudolf Steiner, followed an inner training based on exercises and verses from the path of inner schooling. When he did eventually receive the mantras of the Class Lessons, he clearly stated their source of origin. They were given to him from out of the Michael School.

In our time, so many personal opinions are projected upon these gifts from the path of schooling; even these mantras are often worked with in a dissecting manner. And yet, if we engage with them, they will give to us the substance we need for the deeper schooling. When we adulterate them, even in the name of individuality, they have a different effect.

It is wonderful that so many schooling exercises are available to us, but often we are unable to perceive what we need, or how to work with each given exercise. To admit that we are in schooling is to admit we are spiritually young—to admit that we do not already know is to admit we need the help of those consciousnesses who work to support our growth. This is the 'knock' required upon the 'door' of the School of Michael, in order for it to open to us.

Children are helpless and must accept help from individuals in their surroundings. But gradually they outgrow this helplessness and become helpers in their own circle. The same is true of the grand span of human development in the universe.[52]

There is a reason why esoteric schooling has strict forms; the forms serve not to control but to liberate the human being. They help to 'grow us up.' We need to reach spiritual maturity. No one who has passed with 'seeing' faculties into the elemental world will be able to take this training lightly. For the improperly prepared, the effects of this world can be devastating to the inner balance of the individual's life. The inner work is a 'light on the path,' when properly engaged with. In most esoteric schools, the esoteric exercises are given in the context of an esoteric lesson or knowledge-lesson. A certain soul-preparation forms the right inner attitude for approaching the exercise, verse, or mantra. This also has an effect on the developing soul. "We work together in our groups and gatherings; and through such work not only do we hear certain truths which tell us about the various worlds [...] but by allowing all this to influence us, although we may not always notice it, our soul will gradually change into something different than it was before."[53]

When human beings communicate deeply with one another, they communicate beyond the mere outer content of the words and their physical meaning: they communicate *soul-content*. And those possessing the inner power gained through genuine access to the realms of the spiritual world are able to communicate *soul-activity*. They communicate the *activity of inspiration* from the school in which they themselves are a student. Rudolf Steiner indicated that there was no easier way to develop devachanic organs than through connections *from soul to soul*. "This is why people should be brought together into groups, in order to unite on a purely spiritual basis. It is the will of the Masters to pour life in this way into the stream of humanity. What takes place with the right attitude of mind signifies, for all the members of the group, the opening of a spiritual eye in Devachan."[54]

All who walk the genuine path will thereby have something more to give the world, and this will shine through their individual tasks. On occasion and through karmic consequences some have the task of giving esoteric lessons and training. Most often, what a person gains through this work will simply shine through what they are already doing in the world and, through that, change the world itself. A school teacher who enters into esoteric work will, through this, have more power in their words for the children than a teacher who has not taken hold of their own inner life. A doctor taking up inner work will be so guided that they will be able to stand as a comforter to the sick and to lift the fallen—for they now have the inner capacity to do so, and this extends beyond medical knowledge. All those who are courageously working spiritually into the physical world, are serving in this way.

When in courts of law the deeds of human beings are viewed with the eyes of spiritual perception, when at the bed of the sick the doctor spiritually perceives and spiritually heals, when in the schools the teacher brings spiritual knowledge to the growing child, when in the very streets people think and feel and act spiritually, then we shall have reached our ideal, for spiritual science will have become common knowledge.[55]

We could ask ourselves, as a student of the work: *Would I rather 'see' or serve?* The impulses gained from the inner work always lead to *service*, as long as one has entered into the genuine schooling. Some who enter the genuine schooling may develop organs of perception; but if given a choice, such a one will always view the strength and capacity for *service* as the higher goal.

Through one reason or another, a student of the inner work may never develop these organs of perception, but will nevertheless be able to contribute extensively to the evolution of the whole of humanity through their engagement with the work. For all work in this direction will produce results, and the results we see will be beneficial to the world. Inner training is required for all worlds beyond the physical.

In the physical world, we are at the stage of developing the *consciousness soul*; in our time, it is the development of this element that will lead humanity forward. Those who have dedicated themselves to inner development thereby carry the 'signs' of consciousness-soul development. Even when there has been no formal training in an esoteric schooling, many have still progressed in the development of this element through working rightfully with the inner tasks of the consciousness-soul age.

The development of the consciousness soul will lead to four signs, which individuals carry within themselves; and these signs will then be 'lived into' the life around them. These four signs can be expressed as: 1) *Social understanding*: being able to deeply understand others; 2) *Freedom of thought,* such that beliefs and doctrines, whether of a religious nature or otherwise, are no longer able to grasp the thinking of the individual in an unfree way; 3) *A Recognition and understanding of the spirit working in the world*; 4) A life of *conscious striving* for inner development and for the growth of consciousness.

These are the same four signs that all of humanity must develop in order to advance in the right way before the beginning of the next evolutionary period, in the early part of the 31st century.

There are also signs that the individual will show through the fact of having undergone genuine development in the elemental world at this stage of evolution. This aspect of development does require conscious training, because the physical world alone cannot prepare us for the growth required in this sense. These signs are: 1) *An increased feeling of responsibility*, both inwardly and outwardly; 2) *Greater governance* over one's thinking, feeling, and will-forces; 3) *Ownership of one's shadow or 'double'*; 4) *Willingness to meet karma*.

Some signs of spiritual schooling within the School of Michael are: 1) *Consciously working towards the growth of love*; 2) *Giving of oneself in service to the growth of others*; 3) The capacity for *self-surrender* and the ability to *eliminate one's desire for personal gain*; 4) The ability to embody *an inner attitude of sacrifice*—in other words, *to make sacred* the world in which we live. This is achieved through forming a bridge between the deeds enacted by the spiritual beings of love and the world around us, so that the workings of these beings may flow into our outer lives.

We must work in the right way with the inner schooling if it is to produce these signs within us, which may then become active in the world through us. The schooling in the spiritual world is never-ending; there is no final place to arrive at or to pass beyond. Even after certain steps have been surmounted, we are shown a greater vista of more steps ahead. The schooling is a commitment to continuous learning, giving, and transformation through the development of consciousness, love, and responsibility.

4

PREPARING FOR THE
HIGHER SPIRITUAL WORLD

Many schools and traditions of spiritual development concern themselves only with the teachings of the higher spiritual world, and they amplify the techniques used to reach this world. These teachings, for instance in the Vedanta, not only diminish the physical world as being a realm of '*maya*,' but in addition the elemental world is seen as illusory, and the lower spiritual world with the hosts of hierarchies is seen as a distraction from the true goal.

The goal of such teachings is solely and exclusively to find the 'true I.' In the esoteric training as given in anthroposophy, the approach is different; here it is explained *why* each step on this path is necessary, and it is shown that *the end result of our efforts will be determined by the route we take*. It does matter *how* we get there, just as the artist applying paint to a canvas knows that *how* it is applied, and *with what technique*, will determine the end result. This is why the end result cannot be guaranteed as a single, definite form.

In this stream of the Michaelic schooling, the individual is required to make a commitment to walk through all stages of human development. The 7 × 7 × 7, or the esoteric number of 343, speaks of the seven rounds of the seven globes in the seven phases of planetary evolution.

This can be given in the esoteric schooling as *signs* rather than *numbers*: as a triangle followed by a cross, followed by another triangle, representing to the soul the act of uniting with the '343' evolution of humanity.

At the same time, this is also a commitment to walk *each* of the steps, and not to take shortcuts for our own interest or gain. It is true that human beings, for their own individual self, may indeed leave the wheels of life and death behind them once they have integrated the laws of the higher spiritual world into themselves. However, in order to continue to assist in the progression of humanity, we must walk the path that *all* human beings will have to walk, even though this may be a more difficult path.

The esoteric path is either difficult or it is no path at all![56]

Many traditions concentrate on the stage of crossing the threshold to the higher spiritual world because *it is here* that we find the reality of the true 'I'-being. It is here that the living spiritual reality of our higher consciousness exists. They criticize and avoid the development of *Imaginative* consciousness, which is gained from working through the elemental world; they see it as a waste of time and as an illusory phase.

They likewise avoid the development of *Inspirative* consciousness, regarding it as merely another division between self and other—even though it is developed with higher consciousnesses on the spiritual planes. For these traditions, there is no need to communicate with *any other consciousness* if, as they aspire to confirm and to realize, *nothing other than pure spirit truly is*, or *exists*. They seek solely *Intuitive* consciousness, and this to its highest degree. They seek to *unite as one* with the higher spiritual world, for the drop of individual existence to return to the ocean of pure being.

The Michael School leads the human being consciously, step by step, recognizing the rightful and beneficial time and place of each phase or step on the path. *Imaginative* consciousness works as a deeper capacity of *thinking* on the physical plane; it allows us to think thoughts beyond the everyday, reflective brain-thinking; it allows us to think thoughts that will lead humanity into the future in a helpful way. On the elemental plane, it becomes *conscious picture-consciousness*. The individual can see the thoughts and engage with them, and can 'think in pictures.' By means of this capacity, activities from the realm of the *lower spiritual plane* are able to impress themselves into the human thought-substance, so that *what can be experienced only there* (in the lower spiritual plane) may then come to life in living pictures for human consciousness. The activities attained in the realm of the lower spiritual plane 'impress' themselves into the substance of the elemental world, in order that they may be seen as *pictures*; without this 'impression' process, we would have no 'image-recall' of our time in the lower spiritual plane. The step from reflective thinking to *Imaginative* thinking is a necessary one for human progress. "The creative power of the ego is crippled and devitalized; the self loses strength and can no longer stand up to the world, if it is concerned only with reflective thoughts."

The majority of Rudolf Steiner's esoteric work is given from the schooling of the lower spiritual world: the world of the hierarchies—the progressive spiritual beings who are supporting humanity in its forward evolution. He has even been criticized for the fact that he did not speak of the highest realms; one said that, surely, as a high initiate, he should have spoken of these realms. It has even been questioned whether Steiner achieved the levels reached by some of those who follow the Eastern schooling tradition.

However, it is clear that he crossed into the higher worlds, and that he did so rightly. Every ounce of his energy was given in support of the evolution of others. He sacrificed not only what he had, but also what he could have had. Perceiving what was yet to come for humanity in the future, and the unconscious crossing that was to begin in the 20th century, he did all that could be done to show the true path for our consciousness-soul age.

The *way* and *method* of the preparation and schooling are essential to *how* this experience of crossing into the higher spiritual world will be utilized by the individual student. For the person who is properly prepared, this experience could lead to a dedicated commitment to the further evolution of humanity; for one who is ill-prepared, it could result in a life of self-service. Every step taken through the elemental world and through the lower spiritual world not only develops the capacities required for this path, but also leads closer to certain outcomes that will inevitably be born from the life-changing experiences of the higher spiritual world.

The true, forward-evolving path leads us to the development of consciousness, love, and responsibility. These three evolving capacities are not awakened in the initiates alone. Most perceptive human beings can recognize these three attributes as common—most could say: "I would like to be a conscious, loving, and responsible human being." Perhaps these qualities could even be seen as representing an ideal that the majority of human beings work towards during earthly life.

Regardless of how they are expressed, it is nevertheless true that becoming a conscious, loving, and responsible human being does not seem to be an ideal reserved for 'new age,' 'religious,' or 'spiritual' pursuits; rather, it is a healthy, foundational expression of our humanity.

The essential foundations of consciousness, love, and responsibility are worked with on every plane of existence. In the physical world, this work is expressed in our humanity. We see the manifestation of this work in the unfolding of life and its experiences. Rudolf Steiner states that the spiritual meaning behind all illness and suffering is to help us develop and evolve.[58] From the point of view of the spirit, all things in life exist in order to support the development of these three essential foundations.

As we grow beyond the physical plane by means of this schooling, we encounter another level of the development of consciousness, love, and responsibility in the elemental world. Through the elemental world and all that we have had to experience there, we have learned to be responsible: we have been compelled to take responsibility for our thoughts, feelings, and actions as we have seen the way they influence the elemental substance around us. We have had to gain another level of ego-consciousness in order to develop the 'elemental backbone.' Instead of simply watching our inner soul state, we learn to *take responsibility* for what lives in us. It is often our love for someone close to us that makes us want to change our ugly soul-forms, as we do not want to impose these forms on the other. On this path, we develop *out of love for humanity*. We engage with the hard work of taking hold of ourselves *not* because it suits us, but because of love's gesture of giving to the world; no one would do this work without the influence of love calling them onwards.

If we had not had any inner training, and if we were to be loosened from the physical by some other means, then we would also experience the elemental world. This is beginning to happen naturally for many human beings in the 21st century who are incarnating with some form of inner 'readiness' for further development. How do these individuals cope with such an experience without the eso-teric wisdom that can provide guidance in rightly meet-ing the intensification of the inner life? Many of these people look towards various schools for wisdom, guid-ance and deeper understanding; and a greater presence of the Michaelic schooling could be a beacon of light and strength for them—reminding them of their divine origin and shedding light on a path towards freedom.

If ever your soul is weak, if ever you believe that the goals of earth existence are beyond your reach, think of the human being's divine origin and become aware of those divine forces within you which are also forces of supreme love. Become inwardly conscious of the forces that give you confidence and certainty in all your work, through all your life, now and in all ages of time to come.[59]

Many so-called 'self-development techniques' can have the effect of loosening the soul from the body: for instance, chanting, breathing techniques, and various exercises belonging to earlier stages of human development all have their influence in terms of changing the relationship between body and soul. They lead the individual into other states of consciousness, but they do not serve to prepare in us the tools we need in order to benefit from those experiences—for we have entered into an age in which deeper *self-governance* is necessary.

The use of so-called 'recreational substances' loosens the soul and spirit from the body through toxicity. All substances that produce a 'high' effect are acting to loosen the connection between the soul-spiritual element and the body. They affect how the astral element is able to engage into the nerve-sense system as well as the metabolic system, thus pulling the soul-spiritual out from both. This is different from the effect of *analgesics*, which are used for pain relief; these affect the pain receptors, and they can be seen to work in a comparatively mechanical way, as they do not affect the consciousness of the individual's sense of self. They alter the pain-experience of the body, but *not the consciousness*—unless they are painkillers belonging to forms such as the opiate family, in which case the consciousness is also affected.

If the substance user is lucky, when the toxicity wears off and is excreted by the physical body, the body-soul relationship will return to its normal condition, to how it was before. It thus once again becomes healthily oriented in the sense world. If it does not return to its original state, then we may continue to see disturbances within the inner life of the substance user, even years later.

'Gate-crashing' the spiritual world, for whatever reason one may choose to do this, can have far greater consequences than the possibility of not being able to regain a healthy inner life in the physical world afterwards. If we enter the spiritual world not on the basis of our own preparation and strength, but through other means, then Ahriman can take hold of our 'elemental backbone.' This always leads to a weakening of the ego-hood—not the strengthening that is required for healthy development in our time. If Ahriman has taken hold of our ego, then Lucifer steps in and diverts the soul's petals of perception; the consequence is that we are not able to perceive the true spiritual world, but only the one the forces of egotism want us to see.

Lucifer ties the petals of soul-perception to the elemental backbone. This means *we will only have experiences of our own making*. No genuine training takes place, even if we have so-called 'mystical experiences.' Ahriman is determined to win over this realm of inner activity for himself. The forces of materialism would like to make the spiritual world appear just like the physical, and this is the battle they are now waging. If they were to win this battle, then each individual would have their own personal experience of other realms. Instead of *true development* which will lead to a conscious unifying of humanity, this circumstance will create greater divisions as the *personal self-will* gains a hold in the realm where it should actually be overcome.

If we develop the 'elemental backbone' ourselves, through gaining ego-strength in the course of consistently *ordering and overcoming our inner world,* then the consequence of this is that Ahriman is able to take up a helpful role in the elemental world, gathering together all the pictures of our past shortcomings and errors. The fact of seeing all our untransformed human traits has a deeply disturbing effect on us. But in seeing them, *we thereby know we are not carrying them onwards* into the spiritual world, where our greater schooling will take place. Once these pictures have been gathered together, then the eternal being of the student wears them like a cloak, making them visible to the student. There is no safe 'crossing' without the individual having undergone some form of this experience of encountering the Guardian of the Threshold. Many, however, do not yet 'see' but only 'sense' the Guardian, and this also enables the crossing to be a rightful one.

There are certain 'signs' that the encounter with the double has taken place in the right way. One of them is the *lack of self-credit* the student takes for any step in their own advancement. For after the encounter with the double, it is clear that all of what lives in me *as my own personal doing* is *not* that in me which is advanced, but that which is still in error. Another sign is the painful recognition of *"how little love lives within."* The students are no longer able to wax on about 'unconditional love' and the like, as they now know that, left to the devices of the being that lives as their own double, no such love would come into existence. The third sign is *an ability to know when one's egotism is at work.* It becomes immediately apparent when the element of egotism has acted out or is acting out. The students must now live with this fact all the time, and this painful reflection walks with them in daily life.

Many more people have an encounter with the Guardian than recognize it. Through reading esoteric works, most expect that this encounter will come about in the form of a vision of this other being; but this is only the case if spiritual sight has developed. In the majority of cases, it is only a 'sensing' of the double; but either way, the reality of the encounter leaves its mark on the inner life, and the student remains continually aware of the resulting impressions, even in daily life. For those who have awoken to this 'sensing' of the double without developing it through training, the encounter with the double would likely lead to feelings of deep depression or worthlessness, or constant anxiety—for without esoteric schooling, the Guardian could be mistaken for the deeper *self*.

One thing that can be a great help to the student of the School is the knowledge that the higher 'light' must first have been born before the shadow could have been revealed. The first encounter with the Guardian happens only once the true path has been found. This encouragement can be enough to protect us from feeling the depths of shame, or burning pain, because of what we carry within ourselves. Some experience this shame to such a degree that it inhibits further progress.

The Guardian will be encountered at every level of development.

The inner biography of spiritual development unfolds *as a vortex*—not in a linear way, as appears to be the case for the outer biography. The inner biography also has its relationship to the spiritual year, but it can take more than a year in time to traverse, because passing through it requires the development of faculties, not just outer time. It is seen as a vortex because we seem to pass through the same points, but just at deeper levels of being. Once the student becomes aware of this 'circling around,' it can make the path easier to endure, because we know we have managed to pass through the stage once before and therefore feel a certain confidence that we shall be able, through inner effort, to pass through it once again at its deeper level. However, because it is now on a deeper level, it is always a harder step. We never feel that we are already prepared with the faculties needed for the deeper level, as the faculties are gained only *through each overcoming*; so each step must be surmounted.

The *first point* on the vortex is *conscious activity towards the awakening of a higher step that is to be made inwardly*: that is, towards the *next* step that the student must take on their individual path. This process of growth comes about only by means of our *active engagement* with our inner or outer life, and this requires courage, effort of will, and focus. In the spiritual world, *direction* is important; we must consistently keep an eye on the step we are being trained in if we do not want to waste time. Steadfastness and single-pointedness of purpose help us to accelerate the inner work.

We can come to recognize the step that we need to face because it will show itself, either in our inner life or in our outer life, as a struggle or 'blind-spot' that we keep encountering. We recognize that we do not possess what is needed in order to meet in the right way or transform what is approaching us.

Through the rules of inner training, the striving students will grow towards the tendency not to blame 'the other' when things are difficult inwardly, but will tend rather to actively seek opportunities to work upon themselves. They do not expect *the other person* to correct *their* behavior, nor will they ask the other to act in a way that does not provoke the student's difficult response. They quickly become aware that *if something is suffering within themselves, it is up to the student to work upon it themselves.* So many people wish to condemn the outer 'other' if they feel certain uncomfortable experiences. But the student of the inner work is aware that this reaction only serves to reveal their own unfreedom, and that such a situation is *their own* to do something about.

The clear *second point* on the vortex is *the 'birthing' of a brighter 'light' within*, as something higher, or a new level of the inner life, opens up. This 'clearer light' may also reveal what is to come if we proceed on the rightful path. This may be experienced inwardly as a new level of strength or a new capacity; but often this is overlooked, because the *shadow* cast by the new light also reveals itself, and the student tends to focus on the shadow instead of the newly gained strength.

Many beginning students do not recognize the greater 'light' emerging within themselves. It is worth noting that many are more capable of being aware of the 'darkness' than they are of the 'light.' To use an analogy: In the depths of winter, it is hard to focus on the glow of the small candle flame; but if we take that small flame into a darkened room, then we can see how the darkness no longer exists. However, it takes time to adjust our gaze, as we have become accustomed to the dark; for this reason, our attention is initially drawn to the dark shadows of our inner world. Some students hardly notice the 'light' before the 'shadow' becomes apparent; therefore, they might think that a wrong turn has been made with all the effort they put in, when in fact they have only arrived at the next point of meeting the shadow *because the light has grown stronger,* revealing the next challenge to be faced.

Meeting the shadow within ourselves is the next step in this process. We see what needs to be transformed within us, and what gets in the way of our inner freedom. We should not turn away from this, but enter into it. There is great discomfort in seeing the shadow within, but through seeing the face it is showing, we will be guided to the exact transformations in need of our work and attention.

The *third point* then brings us on towards the *trans-forming-* or *death-process*. The shadow has shown to us what needs transforming, and the students must then apply themselves to this task. We are directed to all that stands in the way of our own greater growth. If we dedicate ourselves to taking on all that thus stands in our way, then this activity will lead us to a breakthrough. At each of these steps, certain inner exercises can be utilized and applied to the process at hand. This not only keeps our focus sharp, but it also allows us to receive the support of the transforming substance of the verse, mantra, or exercise. This will reveal itself as having been successful when, after going through this process, we find that at the next stage of awakening there is more inner light.

The *fourth point* is *integration*, finding ourselves on a new inner level in terms of our capacities and our relationship to the spiritual world. Often this step is overlooked, unless we are able to assess where we have been in comparison to the inner strength we have now gained. In many traditions, this is a time to go backwards over what we have learned in order to ensure that we have learned all we can from it. It is not a time for taking on something new, but for integration and consolidation. It is often not until we 'review the self' that we can recognize just how much has changed inwardly. Along with the changes we undergo in terms of our bearing towards the world—in the sense of no longer reacting to things as being the other person's fault—and along with the increased willingness to meet whatever challenges may arise, we also find a deeper *inner guidance*, which speaks into our lives no longer as a source of direction sounding within at particular times, but as a consistent presence and participator in our inner world.

This integration is followed by the individual's willingness and resolve to keep moving forward; and a new effort is now made, and greater courage is mustered, for the next step. The cycle begins again. At each great cycle of the vortex we meet, and are schooled in, another level of consciousness, love, and responsibility.

The schooling we endeavor to enter is the Michael School, or as it is more widely understood, the School of Love. In deciding to enter this School, we are thereby deciding to work with the beings of progression, and not those seeking to divert humanity. As conscious as we may be in our longing to enter the true School, it is the heart's actual state of purity that is 'read,' not just the wishes or intentions. The principle that *every step of inner development requires three steps in moral development* becomes a truth that reveals itself here.[60]

In the lower spiritual world, the 'sheath-I' gives way to the birth of the 'higher I.' This truly is a momentous step for the student; it becomes a recognition that the way has been found. It is the first true experience of the peace of the 'higher I.'

Along with the 'higher I,' the *soul's capacities* may enter into the lower spiritual world. All true soul-capacities are modifications of *love*. These capacities are what we can give to the world. In the School of Love, they grow and develop.

If we enter the spiritual world rightly, then the diverting force of Lucifer becomes a helper. If we bring with us only the true, the beautiful, and the good—the activity of soul that resounds with the wisdom and harmony of the spiritual world—then Lucifer must assist us by illuminating the soul activity that we bring. This awakens us within the world of spirit; our 'lamp is lit,' and the guiding beings reveal themselves through conversing with the depths of our soul. This 'conversing' does not mean that we listen and then respond; this conversing is an expression of the fact that something is changing in us—as they speak, our soul is transformed. We enter into a schooling that will make true human beings of us. It is only at this point that we can rest in security that the right way has been found.

In the lower spiritual world, we have entered into the School of Love; in having been 'seen,' we are thereby worked with by the progressive beings. The hosts of the hierarchies reveal themselves and continue to train our soul in such a way that it begins to conform to the spirit. We begin to conform to the wisdom and harmony of the School of Love. To be able to live these powers *into the world* and to be responsible for them, is all part of the training. Love becomes not a feeling of sentiment towards others but *deeds* of love.

It was Goethe who exclaimed that the West needs Hafiz; Goethe brought Hafiz to the West. Here, in his poem, "An Enthusiasm to Express Discovery," Hafiz also speaks of this path:[61]

Some painters were engaged in a passionate conversation about the *value of art.*

It was an interesting discussion that I listened to almost an hour without speaking.

Then a young woman turned to me and said, "Any comments, Hafiz?" And these thoughts came to mind that I spoke:

The greatest and most lasting art, the impetus of it, I feel, always comes from wanting to help. A wanting to free, and an enthusiasm to express discovery.

Each soul at some point will begin to feel all is within it and then attends, as it were, to its own inner world. That attendance may not result in anything considered tangible reaching the masses.

But the artist also becomes aware of inner spheres and mingles with them, and then puts those experiences into what they most care about for the world to see and touch if the world wants.

I know all my poems come from a wanting to give something useful.

If at this stage we carry within us what does not belong in this realm, such as our personal desire for gain, then Lucifer has permission to lead us in the direction of a luciferic schooling. Just as Ahriman can take hold of us in the elemental world, deceiving us, so can Lucifer tempt us to enter higher spiritual planes prematurely. It is true that, guided by Lucifer, we may come to know the true order of the spirit—we may see enough to enable us to overcome our own karma and to get off the 'wheels of life and death'—but without the School of Love, all will be done for ourselves, separating us from the collective striving: in that case, my gain will be for me alone. In the School of Love, all power is for serving the other. The only power we may gain in the School of Love is the power to serve others.

If we enter through certain techniques, or 'gate-crash' this world through the use of substances, then it is certainly Lucifer's domain that we enter into. Yet we will have no idea of this. To us, it will be a genuine spiritual experience. To the observer of the spirit, we see greater egotism growing in those individuals even when it is wrapped in altruism and declarations of oneness. Many individuals believe that the taking of recreational drugs has helped them in their relationship to the spirit. Not until their eyes are opened to the genuine path do they recognize the truth for themselves: that it was actually a diversion. Some will argue for years after such substance-induced experiences that it was helpful in preparing for spiritual recognition—until the true path opens, and then they will recognize that it was in fact a hindrance. The only help it can offer us is our ability to recognize it as a false path.

The user of hallucinogenic substance follows this path towards Lucifer. Often this path leads through intense hallucinations of the pictures of the elemental world, and on to a sublime mystical experience; and all of this is achieved through toxins in the body. In our time, even the medical world is studying how hallucinogens can be used to help cancer patients overcome fear. There are several universities working towards this so-called treatment. They are not aware that a quick 'fixing' of the fear today undermines the soul's long-term progress, potentially for lifetimes.

It is in the higher spiritual world that the revelations of consciousness are awoken. In the highest spiritual world, consciousness, love, and responsibility reveal themselves as the archetypes of awakening to the truth and reality of a purely spiritual life. The event is always pure and true, there is no deception possible. In the higher spiritual world, only the higher *is*.

Nothing else exists in the highest spiritual world other than the 'I'. At this point, even the soul-capacities are left behind and dispersed into the cosmos. All that is left is the true 'I', which may now reveal itself within the higher spiritual world, its true home. The experiencing soul is left in the lower spiritual world; at this point, all that exists is consciousness. It is only now that, for the first time, we realize the limitations of the experiencing soul.

We have the possibility of three 'I'-experiences. The first that we experience is the ego or 'sheath-I,' which is developed in the physical world and strengthened to a far greater degree in the elemental world. Then we have the 'higher I,' which is born in the lower spiritual world and develops depth and breadth through the training of the inner schooling of love. There is also the 'true I,' which is only experienced in the great awakening of the higher spiritual world. With the 'true I'-experiences, there is no division between my consciousness and the consciousness of all that is. The 'true I' is pure spirit, and in this realm, only spirit *is*.

To surrender the soul-capacities is extremely difficult, for it is experienced as a 'death' for everything in oneself that can be felt as connected with 'the individual human being.' However, *for the consciousness*, entering into the higher world is not a nebulous death-experience, but *the great awakening*. It becomes not a personal type of 'self-gain,' but a *giving*; as Rumi says, it has not to do with the 'personal you':

Being self-absorbed
you are far from me even in my presence.
Cease to be, for on the path of love
it is either you or me.[62]

Upon *first awakening to the true spirit*, the heights of consciousness are revealed to the candidate of initiation. This experience reveals that *all is one*; there are no 'self' and no 'other' as they exist on other planes. *All is unification in the event of the 'true I.'*

There are three stages of development that show these archetypes of consciousness, love, and responsibility. In the first three 'awakenings' into the higher spiritual world—which will be described below—all is revealed.

The events that take place lead the initiate to a new faculty of experiencing. This is not the 'enduring' of the higher worlds, or 'sensing,' or even 'seeing'; all of these are possible in the other planes. The event of crossing into the higher spiritual world becomes *an indivisible knowing.* What happens takes place on the level where the event and the self are one.

Consciousness is the *first awakening* that leads to the 'true I' event; this awakening will leave a mark on the human soul as the spirit returns back to earthly life. It will leave a mark, which can be 'read' in different ways according to the individual soul's developmental progress before the crossing. For some, it may lead to recognizing the truth of deep esoteric wisdom, such as the Christ's saying, "Truly I say to you, Inasmuch as you have done it to one of the least of these my brothers, you have done it to me."[63] Or it could lead the human being to experience grandiosity of self, extreme self-importance. The feeling of being an 'awakened one' could resound within the soul. How the event resounds in our soul will depend on the soul's preparation. What this soul creates within itself as a result of this event then passes on into the life of the human being. How we act in life is different according to our soul's understanding. Our capacity to give ourselves to life, to the world, comes from the uniting of the soul with the body.

The *second awakening* reveals the *workings of the hierarchies*—not from the details of the lower spiritual world, which is encountered step-by-step—but from the cosmic point of view. As the great 'cosmic clock,' working with impeccable accuracy and timing: thus does the student perceive the workings of the hierarchies. We see the consistent influence of the spirit behind all happenings in the manifested world. We see those who work towards progression and those working to divert humanity, all living within the same spiritual lawfulness that allows them equal permission to influence humanity. The experience of this second crossing can leave its mark on the human soul in different ways, depending on the school in which one has undergone preparation and training. On one hand, the student will feel the deepest commitment to the School of Love, as well as feeling devoted to preparing to become a worthy participant of that School and its activity of working with the progressive beings. On the other hand, if one is not prepared in the right way, this experience can leave the individual feeling as though all people are 'puppets' being pulled and manipulated by higher consciousnesses, and that it does not matter what we do in the world or with whom we align ourselves.

The *third awakening*—this time an awakening of *responsibility*—reveals how the laws of karma become manifest in the world. Here we can learn the laws of how to transform karma and to liberate ourselves from the wheels of life and death. Here, the secrets of the 12 *nidanas*, or 'loops'—which call human beings back into life on earth unless they are *cut through*—are shown to the initiate. For some individual souls, this will lead to an immense feeling of responsibility, and the desire to work with karma in such a way that only the loops are cut which transform personal attachments—but in this sense, the 'consciousness-soul loops' are actually worked with in such a way that we allow them to lead us back into incarnation in order to work with others.

For others, this event will propel within the soul an interest to leave the rounds of life and death as quickly as possible. It will lead to the desire *to work for the self*, in order to lead it away from the world.

The *first loop* is called *avidja* or *ignorance*. In the old schooling, the students would empty themselves of all knowing, arriving at the ability to state "the only thing I know is that I know nothing." For the new schooling we are trained to recognize that the fulfillment of earth evolution will be realized only when we have extracted all possible knowledge from it—that we must traverse the physical world until the awareness of self has absorbed all that the physical world can teach.

The *second loop* is called *sanskara* or *the organizing tendency*. It teaches of the creating of karma, both positive and negative. In some traditions the student is taught to leave no mark, to live in a 'Zen-like' manner, where even your feet do not bruise the grass as they walk on the earth. In the new schooling, the student—for instance a master Mason—would inscribe his 'sign' onto the foundation stone so that he may be drawn back again to that place in future incarnations, in order to continue working with humanity's evolution. All of these experiences can affect the individual being differently, according to how the individual has developed up until the point when the higher crossing occurs.

The fundamental spirit and purpose of development is that one proceeds from taking to giving. [...] Thus, the idea of development moves from a point where one takes, to a point where one streams out, creates. The concept of the 'creator' arises before our spiritual eye, and we may say that every being evolves from creature to creator.[64]

On the true path, a *fourth crossing* is possible. Only those who choose to unite themselves with the earth's evolving stream, and who have committed themselves irrevocably to humanity's development, may achieve it. In the higher spiritual world, the initiate experiences the event of the Mystery of Golgotha. An understanding for the sacrifices that other beings have made for the sake of humanity becomes a fact of experience. In addition, there is an understanding that you too will be asked to lay down your soul-bearing life for the sake of others.

My soul development rested upon the fact that I had stood in spirit before the Mystery of Golgotha in a most inward, most earnest celebration of knowledge.[65]

All processes of awakening into the higher spiritual world have a profound effect upon the soul and life of the individual. It cannot be forgotten, as can so many inner experiences of the lower spiritual world. It is *with* you because it now *is* you. There is no division of self and experience; the self *is* the event.

Each crossing leads to revelations of the spirit, which may take lifetimes for the individual student to 'live through' and 'work into' their external life. The experiences are life-changing, as each crossing *changes who you are* at the level of consciousness, and at the same time *reveals who you have always been.* You can no longer live life or see the world in the same way once you have 'seen' in the higher spiritual world. However, this does not mean that there is no longer an individual personality, destiny, or karma that will continue to unfold. What it does mean is that the eternal is strengthened in us, and this affects how we perceive and live in the world.

As long as we live in a personal relationship with the world, things reveal only what links them with our personality. This, however, is their transitory path. If we withdraw ourselves from our transitory part and live with our feeling of self—our 'I'—[focused] in our permanent part, then our transitory part becomes an intermediary for us. What reveals itself through it is an imperishable, an eternal in the things. The seeker of knowledge must be able to establish this relationship between their own eternal part and the eternal in the things.[66]

We begin to establish this relationship, and through this relationship between ourselves and the eternal in the world, our motives will begin to change. People usually act in the world such that they base their motivations on what satisfies them personally, on what will produce self-gain; they place their personality upon the world. The personality, the self-will, does not consciously act in harmony with the spiritual world.

This ability to act out of one's inner being can only be an ideal towards which the seeker strives. The attainment of the goal lies in the far distance, but the seeker of knowledge must have the will to recognize clearly this road. This is the seeker's will to freedom, for freedom is action out of one's inner being. Only that person may act out of their inner being who draws their motives from the eternal.[67]

The world that appears outside us—the physical-sense world—can be seen as the 'dead skin' of the elemental world. The elemental world is the thought-life of a myriad of beings, beings who live and act in the lower spiritual world, the *'Kingdom of God.'* They act, live, and communicate within the lower spiritual world, but their consciousness belongs to the higher realms of consciousness, just as ours does.

It is Michael's task to lead the human being back up again on those paths of will down which they had once come, when they descended with their earthly consciousness on paths of thought from the experience of the supersensible to the experience of the sensory.[68]

What we see behind the physical realm originates in the higher spiritual world, is 'detailed' in the lower spiritual world, and is 'pictured' in the elemental world—then it becomes *manifest* in the physical world. The bridge we have taken to the highest realms is the same bridge that was used in bringing the spirit down into the earthly life. The world we see around us is a product of this higher world. Building the bridge well is essential to being able to bring the revelations of the spirit into earthly activity. Why would we rise up if we were unable to 'bring down' and participate in the evolution of the world? Love for humanity and its evolving journey gives the student of the spirit the only true reason to walk this path rightly. It is difficult and arduous to dedicate the living of one's life to the path.

There can be no question of regarding the esoteric path as a mere adjunct to life; one's path of life must be completely filled with esoteric impulses.[69]

When we come back to our verse, we see that the highest is named and pointed to as a 'true I' reality. In this verse, one of the higher truths is revealed that works on so many levels of our development.

More radiant than the sun,
Purer than the snow,
Finer than the ether
Is the self,
Spirit in my heart.
I am this self,
This self am I.[70]

The student of the higher worlds knows this to be true of the *true self* within each human being. This verse does not speak to us personally; it only speaks the truth. It speaks of the truth that sets us free.

When the first crossing into the higher spiritual world has been achieved, the students now know for themselves, *"I am this self."* This event changes us, and if the bridge has been built step-by-step, it will change what we will be able to bring back across this bridge in order to give to the world. In the depths of our love for humanity, we wish for everyone to know this true self.

When with this great vista of divine ordering of the world—of the revelation, the glory of the heavens—we think of the future lying before humankind, we have a premonition even now of the harmony that in the future will reign in those who know that the more abundantly the harmony of the cosmos fills the soul, the more peace and concord will there be upon the earth.[71]

The path that will lead humanity onwards is the same path that takes us through the various steps and stages, progressing one step at a time. It is our conscious development and embodiment of each of these steps that produces greater and greater harmony, clearing the chaos, and thus serving to make clear the way for others in the world. This 'making clear of the way' will also change the way others are able to embark on the path ahead.

Notes

The quotations from Rudolf Steiner's works cited in the text have been edited to reflect gender-inclusive language.

With grateful acknowledgment to Daniel Landinsky for the use of excerpts from his poetry translations as noted below.

Introduction

1. Rudolf Steiner, CW [Collected Works, Vol.] 267, *Soul Exercises: Word and Symbol Meditations* (Gt. Barrington: SteinerBooks, 2014), p. 32 (Spring 1905, Archive No. 6915-18).

2. Rudolf Steiner, CW 145, *The Effects of Esoteric Development* (New York: Anthroposophic Press, 1997), lecture of 29 March 1913, p. 200.

3. Rudolf Steiner, CW 145, *The Effects of Esoteric Development* (op. cit.), 29 March 1913, p. 200.

4. "You have no idea how unimportant is all that the teacher says or leaves unsaid on the surface, and how important what they themselves are as teacher." Rudolf Steiner, CW 317, *Education for Special Needs: The Curative Education Course* (Forest Row: Rudolf Steiner Press, 2014), lecture 2: 26 June 1924. This translation adapted from the earlier Adams translation of *Curative Education* (London: Rudolf Steiner Press, 1972).

Chapter 1

5. Rudolf Steiner, *Some Conditions for Understanding Supersensible Knowledge*, lecture of 18 January 1920, CW 196. Printed in *The Golden Blade*, 1960; translation adapted.

6. See the chapter on "Continuity of Consciousness" in: Rudolf Steiner, CW 10, *Knowledge of the Higher Worlds and Its Attainment* (New York: Anthroposophic Press, 1947); also printed as *Knowledge of the Higher Worlds: How is it Achieved?* (London: Rudolf Steiner Press, 1993), and *How to Know Higher Worlds* (Gt. Barrington: Anthroposophic Press, 1994).

7. "I implore you—and have implored you in Berlin—to accept nothing that I have ever said or will say on authority or faith. Even before a person reaches the stage of clairvoyance, he has the opportunity to test what has been won through clairvoyant observation [...] Therefore, it follows that the statements made out of the source of Rosicrucianism should not be believed, but examined—not superficially [...] but ever more conscientiously and diligently [...] The more you analyze, the more you will find that what has been said from out of this source demonstrates its own truth. You should take nothing on authority." Rudolf Steiner, CW 121, *The Mission of the Folk Souls* (Forest Row: Rudolf Steiner Press, 2005), lecture of 17 June 1910.

8. Rudolf Steiner, CW 26, *Anthroposophical Leading Thoughts* (London: Rudolf Steiner Press, 1973), "The Human Being in His Macrocosmic Nature," p. 193, translation adapted.

9. Rudolf Steiner, CW 10, *Knowledge of the Higher Worlds and Its Attainment* (op. cit.), Chapter: "Some Practical Aspects," pp. 105-106, tr. Metaxa/Monges; *Knowledge of the Higher Worlds: How is it Achieved?* (op. cit.), pp. 97-98, rev. tr. Davy/Osmond.

10. "I have a dream that my four children will one day live in a nation where they will not be judged by the color of their skin, but by the content of their character." Speech of 28 August 1963, delivered at the Lincoln Memorial, Washington D.C. (Quoted from: http://www.americanrhetoric.com/speeches/mlkihaveadream.htm).

11. Rudolf Steiner, CW 135, *Reincarnation and Karma* (London: Rudolf Steiner Press, 1977; Gt. Barrington: SteinerBooks, 2001), lecture of 21 February 1912.

12. Descriptions of the exercise can be found in: Rudolf Steiner, CW 266a, *Esoteric Lessons, 1904–1909: From the Esoteric School* (Vol. 1) (Gt. Barrington: SteinerBooks, 2011), Hamburg, 22 May 1908.

13. See, for example, the Translator's Note at the end of G. and M. Adams' translation of *Occult Science: An Outline* (London: Rudolf Steiner Press, 1979, p. 331): "In earlier translations, *Bewusstseinsseele* had been rendered more literally: 'consciousness-soul.' Dr. Steiner subsequently gave 'spiritual soul' as the true equivalent."

14. Rudolf Steiner, *The Festivals and Their Meaning* (London: Rudolf Steiner Press, 1996), lecture: "Whitsun: The Festival of Free Individuality," CW 118, 15 May 1910, translation adapted.

15. Rudolf Steiner, CW 207, *Cosmosophy, Vol. 1* (New York: Anthroposophic Press, 1985), lecture of 8 October 1921.

16. Rudolf Steiner, *How Can the Destitution of Soul in Modern Times Be Overcome? Social Understanding, Liberty of Thought, Knowledge of the Spirit*, lecture of 10 October 1916 in Zurich. From CW 168; reprinted at RSArchive.org.

17. Hafiz, *I Heard God Laughing: Poems of Hope and Joy* (NY: Penguin Books, 2006), trans. Daniel Ladinsky, p. 8.

18. Rudolf Steiner, CW 245, *Guidance in Esoteric Training: From the Esoteric School* (London: Rudolf Steiner Press, 2001), p. 81.

CHAPTER 2

19. Rudolf Steiner, CW 26, *Anthroposophical Leading Thoughts* (op. cit.), Leading Thought #170, pp. 194-195, translation adapted.

20. J. W. v. Goethe. For the full quotation and source, see the heading to Chapter 3 on p. 81.

21. Hafiz, *The Subject Tonight is Love: 60 Wild and Sweet Poems of Hafiz* (NY: Penguin Books, 2003), trans. Daniel Ladinsky, p. 56.

22. Rudolf Steiner, CW 134, *The World of the Senses and the World of the Spirit* (Forest Row: Rudolf Steiner Press, 2014), lecture of 31 December 1911, translation adapted.

23. Rudolf Steiner, CW 10, variously translated: *Knowledge of the Higher Worlds and Its Attainment* (op. cit.); *Knowledge of the Higher Worlds: How is it Achieved?* (op. cit.); *How to Know Higher Worlds* (op. cit.).

24. Rudolf Steiner, CW 245, *Guidance in Esoteric Training* (op. cit.), p. 81.

25. For example, Peter Deunov (1864–1944), Bulgarian teacher of Esoteric Christianity: "When the spirits of those [animals] killed pass into the astral world, they create the conditions for the diseases of the nervous system in human beings. You think that

when you kill a lamb, you do not bear responsibility. The lamb is guided by the Advanced Beings, and these caregivers of the lamb will ask for an account of its life. Today these Beings may keep their silence, but one day you will become accountable for all your actions. The suffering of mammals is great: more than one hundred million mammals are killed each year. Great slavery exists in this; there is no law to protect them. The nervous disorders of the white race today are a result of the killing of animals. At their time of slaughter, fear and repugnance develop in the animals. As a result of this, unfavorable conditions for human development are formed in the astral world." (Peter Deunov, *The Wellspring of Good: The Last Words of the Master Peter Deunov.* Kibea 2002. Ed. B. Boav and B. Nikolov.)

26. Douglas Sloan, *The Redemption of the Animals: Their Evolution, Their Inner Life, and Our Future Together. An Anthroposophic Perspective* (Gt. Barrington: Lindisfarne, 2015).

27. Hafiz, *A Year with Hafiz: Daily Contemplations* (NY: Penguin Books, 2010), trans. Daniel Ladinsky, entry of June 18, p. 92.

28. Rudolf Steiner, *Some Conditions for Understanding Supersensible Knowledge*, lecture of 18 January 1920, CW 196 (op. cit.), translation adapted.

29. Rudolf Steiner often describes the *double* in relation to the experience of the *Guardian of the Threshold*. In one of his more concise descriptions, he says that at a certain stage of initiation, "[...] there arises the phenomenon known as the Guardian of the Threshold—the appearance of the *lower double* of the human being. The spiritual organism of the human being, composed of their impulses of will, desires, and thoughts, appears to the initiate in visible form. It is a form that is sometimes repugnant and terrible, for it is the offspring of one's good and bad desires and of one's *karma*—it is their personification in the astral world, the *evil pilot* of the Egyptian Book of the Dead. This form must be conquered by the human being before they can find the higher self." Rudolf Steiner, CW 94, *An Esoteric Cosmology* (Gt. Barrington: SteinerBooks, 2008), Lecture VIII, 1 June 1906. For descriptions of further aspects of the "double," see

also *Knowledge of the Higher Worlds* (op. cit), Chapter: "The Guardian of the Threshold"; *An Outline of Occult Science*, Chapter V: "Knowledge of the Higher Worlds" (Monges trans., Spring Valley: Anthroposophic Press, 1972 / also available as *Occult Science: An Outline*, Adams trans., London: Rudolf Steiner Press, 1979); and the lecture of 16 November 1917 in CW 178, *Geographic Medicine and the Mystery of the Human Double* (Spring Valley, NY: Mercury Press, 1986).

CHAPTER 3

30. Goethe, *Scientific Studies. Goethe: The Collected Works, Vol. 12* (Princeton University Press, 1995), p. 164.

31. "[The seeker] eliminates the element of self in order that pleasure and joy from the outer world may work on in them" (*Theosophy*, ibid., p. 164).

32. Rudolf Steiner, CW 9, *Theosophy* (New York: Anthroposophic Press, 1971), Ch. 4: "The Path of Knowledge," p. 165, tr. H. Monges/G. Church, translation adapted.

33. Rudolf Steiner, *Some Conditions for Understanding Supersensible Knowledge*, lecture of 18 January 1920, CW 196 (op. cit.), translation adapted.

34. Lisa Romero, *The Inner Work Path: A Foundation for Meditative Practice in the Light of Anthroposophy* (Gt. Barrington: SteinerBooks, 2014).

35. Rudolf Steiner, CW 147, *Secrets of the Threshold* (Gt. Barrington: SteinerBooks, 2007), lecture of 29 August 1913.

36. Mabel Collins, *Light on the Path* (Pasadena: Theosophical University Press, 1997), p. 1.

37. Rudolf Steiner, *Four Mystery Dramas* (Gt. Barrington: SteinerBooks, 2014), Second Drama: "The Guardian of the Threshold," words of Lucifer.

38. Rudolf Steiner, CW 177, *The Fall of the Spirits of Darkness* (London: Rudolf Steiner Press, 1995), lecture of 26 October 1917.

39. Rudolf Steiner, CW 316, *Course for Young Doctors* (Spring Valley, NY: Mercury Press, 1994), lecture of 9 January 1924.

40. Rudolf Steiner, CW 245, *Guidance in Esoteric Training* (op. cit.), p. 81.

41. Rudolf Steiner, CW 245, *Guidance in Esoteric Training* (op. cit.), p. 81.

42. Rudolf Steiner, CW 147, *Secrets of the Threshold* (op. cit.), lecture of 28 August 1913.

43. See Rudolf Steiner, CW 238, *Karmic Relationships, Vol. IV* (London: Rudolf Steiner Press, 1983), 28 September 1924, p. 171.

44. Tallapragada Subba Row (1856–1890): Prominent member of the Theosophical Society and author of several books on ancient wisdom.

45. Rudolf Steiner, CW 245, *Guidance in Esoteric Training* (op. cit.), p. 81.

46. Rabindranath Tagore, *Stray Birds* (New York: The Macmillan Company, 1916), verse 135.

47. Rudolf Steiner, CW 10, *Knowledge of the Higher Worlds and Its Attainment* (op. cit.), Chapter: "The Stages of Initiation," pp. 44-45, tr. Metaxa/Monges; *Knowledge of the Higher Worlds: How is it Achieved?* (op. cit.), pp. 51-52, rev. tr. Davy/Osmond, trans. adapted.

48. Descriptions of this meditation can be found in: *Rudolf Steiner, CW 266c, Esoteric Lessons, 1913–1923: From the Esoteric School, Vol. 3* (Gt. Barrington: SteinerBooks, 2011), May 1923.

49. Rudolf Steiner, CW 267, *Soul Exercises: Word and Symbol Meditations* (op. cit.), Archive No. 3214. In German: *Seelenübungen, Band I* (Dornach, 2001), p. 217.

50. Rudolf Steiner, *A Social Basis of Education* (Steiner Schools Fellowship Publications, 1994), Stuttgart, lecture of 8 June 1919 (Whitsun), CW 192. This translation is from the German edition: *Geisteswissenschaftlicher Behandlung sozialer und pädegogischer Fragen* (Dornach 1991), p. 149.

51. Thomas Aquinas, "On Behalf of Love," in: *Love Poems from God: Twelve Sacred Voices from the East and West* (NY: Penguin Books, 2002), trans. Daniel Ladinsky, pp. 123-124.

52. Rudolf Steiner, CW 110, *The Spiritual Hierarchies and the Physical World* (Gt. Barrington: SteinerBooks, 2008), lecture of 13 April 1909, evening.

53. Rudolf Steiner, *Nature Spirits: Selected Lectures* (Forest Row: Rudolf Steiner Press, 1995), lecture of 3 April 1912, p. 20, translation adapted.

54. Rudolf Steiner, CW 93a, *Foundations of Esotericism* (London: Rudolf Steiner Press, 1983), notes to a course of esoteric lessons: lecture of 9 October 1905.

55. Rudolf Steiner, *The Festivals and Their Meaning* (op. cit.), lecture: "The Christmas Festival: A Token of the Victory of the Sun," 24 December 1905, translation adapted.

CHAPTER 4

56. Rudolf Steiner, CW 316, *Course for Young Doctors* (op. cit.), lecture of 6 January 1924.

57. Rudolf Steiner, CW 58, *Transforming the Soul, Vol. 1* (London: Rudolf Steiner Press, 2005), lecture of 22 October 1909, p. 63.

58. See Rudolf Steiner, CW 120, *Manifestations of Karma* (Forest Row: Rudolf Steiner Press, 2012).

59. Rudolf Steiner, CW 127, *The Festivals and Their Meaning* (op. cit.), "The Birth of the Sun Spirit as the Spirit of the Earth," lecture of 26 December 1911.

60. "For this reason, all who seek to discover through personal vision the secrets in human nature must follow the golden rule of true spiritual science. This golden rule is as follows: *For every one step that you take in the pursuit of higher knowledge, take three steps in the perfection of your own character.*" Rudolf Steiner, CW 10, *Knowledge of the Higher Worlds and Its Attainment* (op. cit.), Chapter: "The Stages of Initiation," pp. 68-69, tr. Metaxa/Monges; *Knowledge of the Higher Worlds: How Is It Achieved?* (op. cit.), p. 70, rev. tr. Davy/Osmond.

61. Hafiz, *A Year with Hafiz: Daily Contemplations* (op. cit.), entry of June 19, pp. 93-94.

62. Rumi, *Rumi's Little Book of Life* (Hampton Roads, 2012), trans. M. Mafi and A.M. Kolin, p. 164.

63. Matthew 25:40. American King James Version.

64. Rudolf Steiner, CW 110, *The Spiritual Hierarchies and the Physical World* (op. cit.), lecture of 13 April 1909, evening.

65. Rudolf Steiner, CW 28, *Autobiography: Chapters in the Course of My Life* (Gt. Barrington: SteinerBooks, 2006), Chapter 26. Quoted from S.O. Prokofieff, *The Mystery of the Resurrection in the Light of Anthroposophy* (Forest Row: Temple Lodge, 2010), p. 154.

66. Rudolf Steiner, CW 9, *Theosophy* (op. cit.), Ch. 4: "The Path of Knowledge," p. 172, translation adapted.

67. Rudolf Steiner, Ibid., p. 175, translation adapted.

68. Rudolf Steiner, CW 26, *Anthroposophical Leading Thoughts* (op. cit.), Leading Thought #105, p. 70, translation adapted.

69. Rudolf Steiner, CW 316, *Course for Young Doctors* (op. cit.), lecture of 6 January 1924.

70. Rudolf Steiner, CW 245, *Guidance in Esoteric Training* (op. cit.), p. 81.

71. Rudolf Steiner, *The Festivals and Their Meaning* (op. cit.), lecture: "The Christmas Festival: A Token of the Victory of the Sun," 24 December 1905, translation adapted.

LISA ROMERO is a complementary health practitioner and adult educator, who has applied anthroposophy to her practice since 1990 and delivered education enriched with anthroposophy since 1998. The primary focus of her work since 2006 has been teaching inner development and anthroposophical meditation. Her first book on the inner work, *The Inner Work Path – A Foundation for Meditative Practice in the Light of Anthroposophy,* was published in 2014; *Developing the Self – Through the Inner Work Path in the Light of Anthroposophy* was published in 2015.

Lisa lectures and presents courses and retreats on the inner work and anthroposophical meditation for professional and personal development. These are offered throughout the year in many communities worldwide. Lisa's capacity to deliver esoteric wisdom with insight and understanding allows her to meet the diverse needs of communities and professions.

For several years, Lisa was the lecturer for Health and Nutrition and Male/Female Studies at Sydney Rudolf Steiner College, where she now continues to lecture the tutors on inner development. She also designed and facilitated the Educaredo Towards Health and Healing course. This training ran eight, year-long courses working with therapists from all modalities, as well as Waldorf teachers, to bring the practical application of therapeutic and pedagogical methods. She continues to teach in numerous trainings and seminars for several organizations.

Essentially, Lisa's work springs from the inner work, meditation, and exercises, together with a dedication to the path of unfolding consciousness. She brings a depth of insight that is reflected in the experiences and changes in the participants who share in this work.

FOR INFORMATION ON COURSES AND CLASSES
CONTACT LISA ROMERO AT :

innerworkpath.com